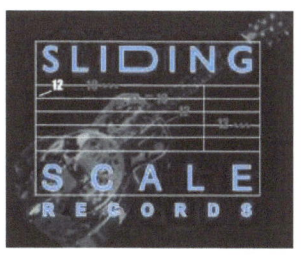

slidingscale.co.uk

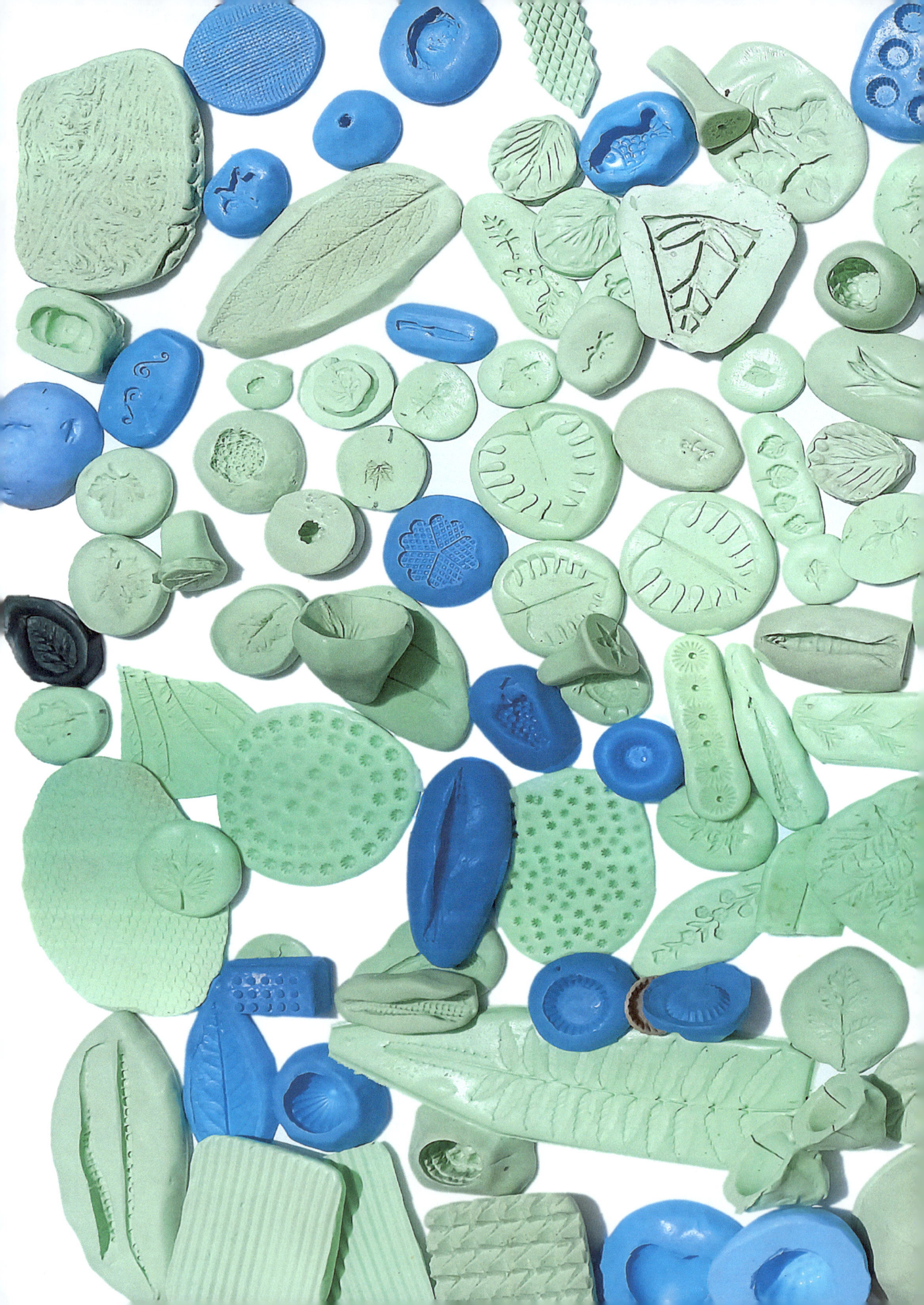

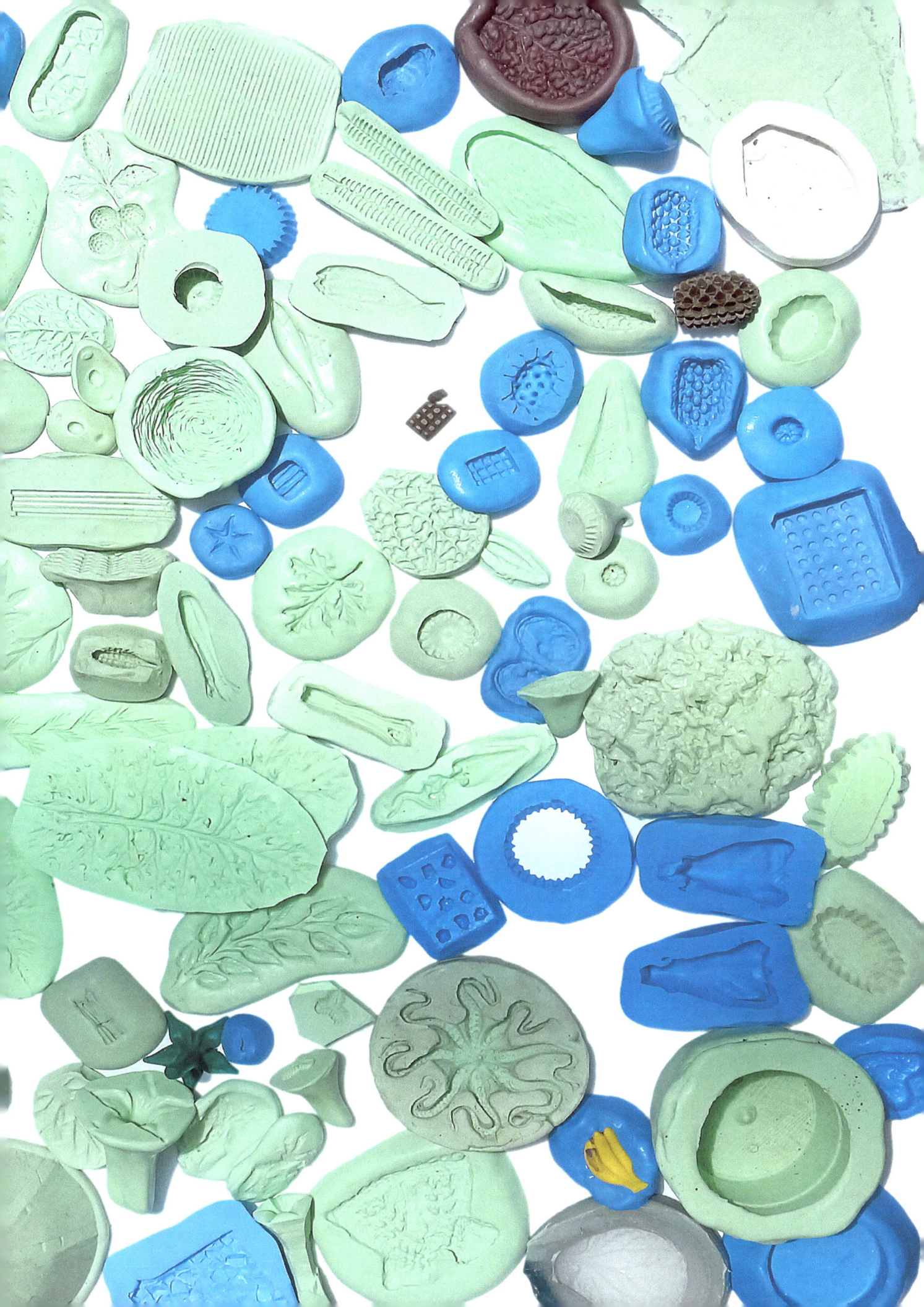

Peace lily 'fruit' for miniature Kiwano melon

Simple Mold Making

Quick molding ideas for miniaturists, model makers and animators.

Angie Scarr

Dedication

Dedicated to all my Patreon patrons, both those who are listed on the thanks page and the anonymous ones. Without you this book would never have seen the light of day. Thank you!

Publishing Data

First edition published 2022 (SSPB13)

Text copyright Angie Scarr

Illustration, composites and photographs copyright Frank Fisher, Angie Scarr

Design by Frank Fisher, Angie Scarr

Plaza De Andalucía 1, Campofrío, 21668, Huelva, Spain.

ISBN 9798840543238

All rights reserved. No part of this book may be reproduced, or transmitted in any form or by any means without the express permission of the copyright owners.

The right of Angie Scarr to be identified as the author of this work has been asserted in accordance with the Copyright Designs and Patents Act 1988, sections 77 & 78.

No part of this publication may be reproduced, stored in a retrieval system or transmitted in any form or by any means without the prior permission of the publisher and author or her agents

Descriptions of sales and advertising platforms are for information purposes only and are not recommendations. The authors can accept no responsibility for the application of any information contained in this book. Further, no responsibility is implied or accepted for current or future application of social media and data collection laws.

The publishers and author can accept no legal responsibility for any consequences from the application of information instructions or advice given in this publication.

Contents

Intro	5
What is 2 part silicone mould material?	6
Why use 2 part silicone moulding paste?	6
Other tools and materials	6
Polymer clay	7
Sculpting tools	7
Intro to moulding uses and principles	8
What can you use moulding for?	8
Why use moulded items in your work?	10
How to mix	12
What can you mould from?	12
Beginners quick start project	14
Borrowing forms from everyday objects	16
Simple texture plates	16
Griddle plate project	16
Moulds from your own work	18
Dabbers printers and impression tools	18
Words — soap	18
Parmesan and parma ham stamps	19
Moulds from fabric	22
2 Part crochet bunny mould	24
Moulding from nature	27
The generous plant world	28
Flexible moulds (for leaf veiners etc.)	28
Simple leaf veiners	28
Imprinters leaf project	30
Mushrooms	32
Making a scene with moulds	33
Fish mould projects	34
Squid mini project	34
Fish fillets & kipper	35
Crabs, lobsters and crayfish	36
Octopus mould project	37
Using a wavy blade: seaweed	40
Making a mini scallop shell mould	41
To make your scallops	41
Oysters	43
Moulding reference charts	45
Moulds for setting liquid materials	56
Project: how to make a master set of false teeth for moulding in liquid fimo	58
Flexible formers	61
Basket former	62
How to use a basket former	62
Hanging basket and planters project	64
How to make a hat former	64
Almost impossibly difficult shapes	66
Bathroom set moulds project	68
Extrusion techniques	69
Copyright issues - moulds	70
Moulds for surface effects	71
Using moulding and pressed patterns	72
Miniature ceramic or faux cast iron	72
Problem solver	75
Suppliers	77
Biog, thanks & acknowledgements	78
Index	79
Patreon	80
Catalogue of Sliding Scale books	81
Contact and social media	82

4

Intro

This book aims to make a complex subject easy and accessible to all, with the minimum of outlay. Hopefully it will also open your mind to the many possibilities for 'borrowing' the sculpting work nature provides you with, adding little bits of shapes from other items you find around the house or your workshop and coming up with loads of ideas of your own. Although I work in polymer clay many of these hacks are also useful for other materials.

Even though I've written several books which have included making moulds within them, I've never concentrated on this side of my work. I now intend to dispel any idea that making moulds is somehow cheating or uncreative. I believe it's just another tool for bringing your own creativity to life and making repetition of forms possible where otherwise the process of repeating items or elements would be unbearably dull. An item made using a mould certainly has no lesser value. If you believe it does, ask the people who own the latest Apple iPhone! So let's go on a journey of possibilities, sometimes into creating super reality and illusion in very small scale with the help that moulds can give you.

You don't have to be a master mould maker to get real fun and a serious creative boost from making your own moulds for your craft work. Although I use polymer clays and related materials, of course you can use these moulds not only for polymer clay but also for plaster casting, pottery and even edibles such as fondant and chocolate. Check that the mould material you are using is food safe though, and always wash new silicone moulds before using for any edible items. You should definitely not mix uses of the same mould!

A note on language. We have used the American spelling 'mold' in the title because our demographic leans that way, but I'm a British English native speaker and I felt it would be more authentic to speak with my own natural voice. Apologies if this causes any confusion. Having 'polled' my Patreon patrons, they seem to approve of the compromise: and I trust them.

What is 2 part silicone mould material?

There are many brands available but essentially they all share the same or similar properties. They are 'silicone rubber' materials which set, but remain flexible.

Technically they are actually known as 'addition vulcanising'. This means that, like certain glues and resins, they are reasonably stable until the two parts are put together. I say reasonably because they do have a shelf life, usually about 2 years, after which its setting ability cannot be guaranteed.

We use our own Minitmold brand because it is fast set and flexible, but other brands will work and some are cheaper. You may prefer slower-setting or less flexible materials. Experiment to find what suits you.

It's so simple to use and there are so few mistakes that can be made it's easy to learn even for children and people with learning difficulties and yet when mastered the results can be as good as any other mould under most circumstances.

It's very flexible so you can have a slight undercut which is not possible with more solid materials.

Carrot base layer with undercut

My advice to the curious artist is always to keep a pair of pots of the 2 part moulding material in your pocket or handbag. You'll be surprised when inspiration hits you!

See the middle pages for easy reference as to where to find shapes.

Other tools and materials

Found materials for textures and shapes. Loads of these are mentioned throughout the book and can be found in the handy reference in the middle of the book too.

2 part materials in separate containers

Why use 2 part silicone moulding paste?

Because it is so quick you can see the results of your work almost instantly. If there are any errors you can do the work again straight away.

Wooden domes

Textures from the natural world

Polymer clay

You can use any clay for the projects that don't require complex sculpting but where you need really good detail I recommend ProSculpt. Although I've used brown in some cases for photography reasons, the colour is actually unimportant. Puppenfimo is also good.

I've presupposed that you have used polymer clay before so haven't covered basic principles of using and baking polymer clay. If you have never used it before you do need to read all the instructions on the packet really well. Follow all temperature guidance. Of course I'll recommend my books especially if you're a miniaturist!

Sculpting tools

Ball tools, wax carving tools, silicone painting tools, hand modelling tools, a blackhead remover (looks like a little scoop with a hole in it), dental tools, and smoothing tools. And various shapes of small cutters are all useful. I also collect leather punches and leather cutting and embossing tools.

Collect shapes and textures for your own texture tool collection.

Of course, I have collected my tools and shapes over many years. You don't need to start with anything like this many. A couple of dental tools and a couple of ball tools will get you started. The fun is keeping your eyes open for items that might be useful and inspire you.

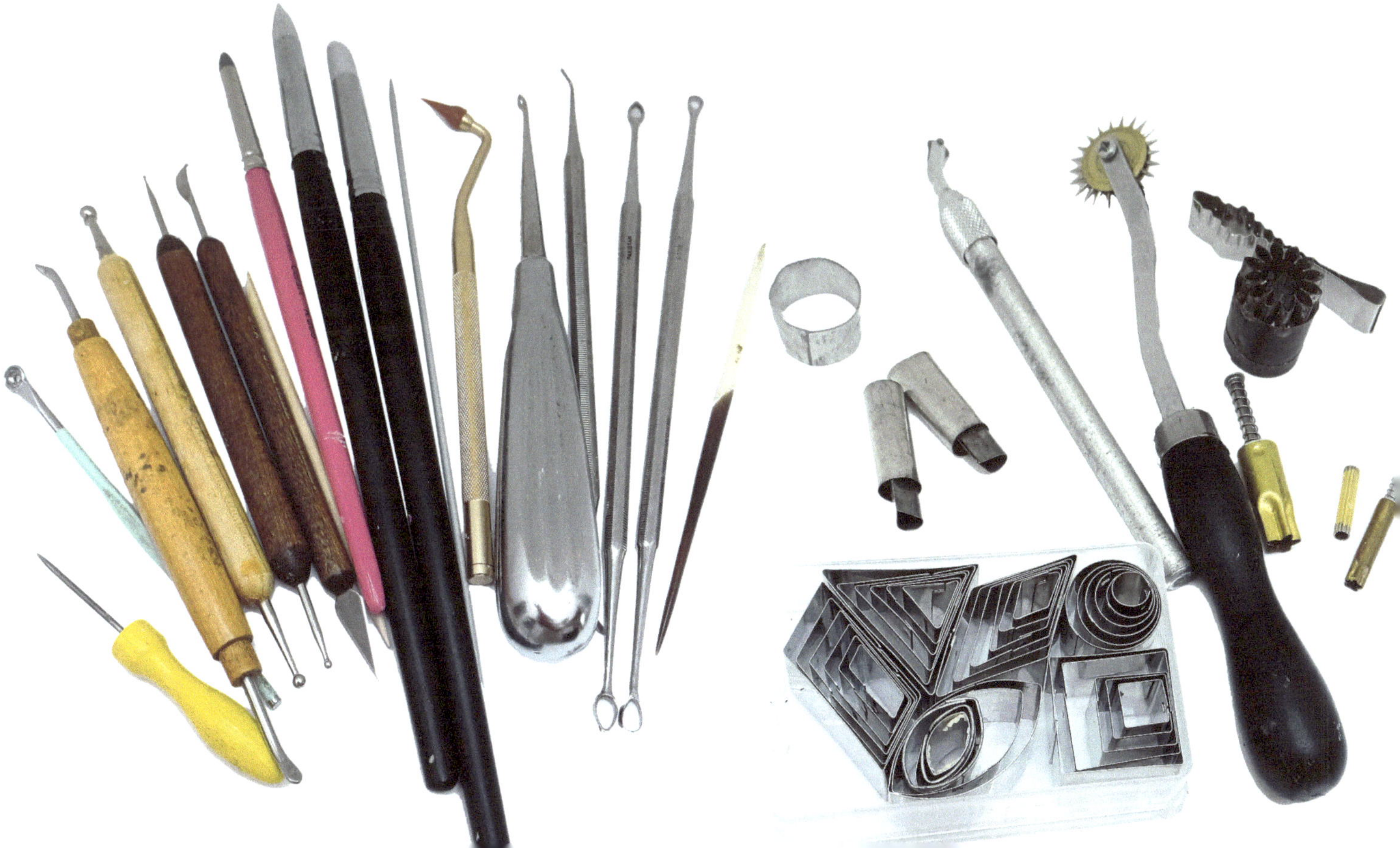

Intro to moulding uses and principles

A few recommendations for making moulds

Before you start, if at all possible, you should have clean hands and a clean work surface. If you're out 'in the field' this may not be possible.

Firstly, especially if you are using a super fast setting material, be ready with the exact item you want to mould from before you start mixing. If you aren't ready the mix will go off before you find it. Once you have started making a mould remember not to answer the door, or the phone or the call of nature until you're ready to leave the mould to set. Your material might go off before it's properly shaped and will be useless. All mould making materials of any quality are expensive and so it's a great idea to start with small unimportant items like moulding from small leaves etc.

Check your mould or the first side of your mould before you continue. Look for shiny patches. Any shiny bits could mean air has got between the object and the mould. Throw away this part and start again.

The golden rules of mould making

•	An imperfect master can never make a perfect mould

•	And an imperfect mould will never produce a perfect replica.

•	A badly mixed material will make for an easily damaged mould.

•	Shiny patches in your mould indicate that air bubbles have got in.

•	Simplify and exaggerate the 'essence' of an item to make up for the fact that some definition can be lost in the mould making and then in repeat production from that mould.

If your mould is wrong or disappointing don't try and salvage it unless the original is broken and you have no alternative. Start again. A poor mould will never be a good mould.

Be aware moulding in liquid polymer and baking in the mould (covered later) requires that you wash the mould really thoroughly as the residue on a freshly made silicone mould can react with polymer clay in the baking process to produce a crumbly surface.

What can you use moulding for?

As a miniaturist I've used moulds for creating and re-creating miniature forms. Of course

Hand made spring onions and making the mould

you can also use any of these forms for jewellery parts, pieces for artwork, resin art and cake decoration. Almost all silicone mould materials are non toxic or considered food safe. Check your packet for food safety status and always wash a mould really well in washing up liquid and water and rinse very well before using for edible work.

You can also use moulded work for architects models, railway modelling, mask making, maquettes and even animation, especially stop motion animation. You can use in mathematics and language education to make repeats of items in different colours.

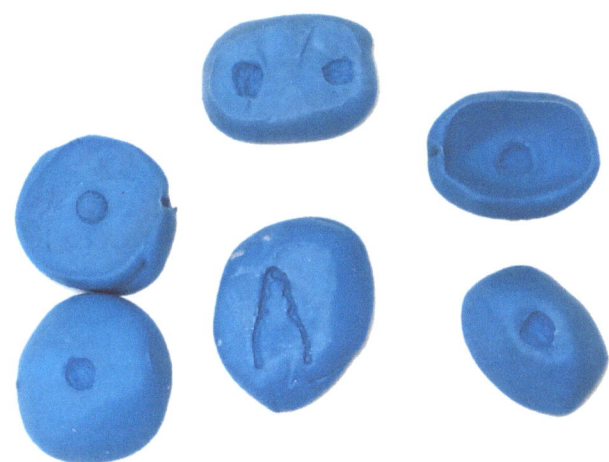

Mould of nutcracker by Andrew Gregory

Archiving: for example If there is some work that will never again be repeated. If it's too difficult and complicated (see moulds for almost impossibly difficult shapes) or if the artist is no longer with us but you want to pay tribute to their work. I have saved a mould of a wonderful little nut cracker by my friend Andrew Gregory. Andrew is sadly no longer with us and so I can't find any more of his lovely nutcrackers. So I saved a mould of my last set in case I ever need to make them again. In a case like this you would always credit the original.

Master artists in the worlds of miniatures, jewellery and art objects often use moulding in their work. Not all of them admit it, but it shouldn't be considered a cheat or an inferior form of working because it is just another tool to help you make better work with a more predictable but not necessarily the same outcome.

Everything you produce from that mould initially looks the same. But because you can manipulate the final form after moulding infinitely, you can use moulding simply as a shortcut for a first stage in sculpting. Of course for some arts, moulding can be vital.

Top tips: silicone moulding in the field

Be sure you know what you are going to take a mould from, which way up it's going to be, and how many parts you will need the mould to be in before you start to mix. You can't waste time. The better mould making materials begin to cure within a couple of minutes so you have no time to re-do mistakes.

Moulded 'pebble' to make miniature rocks

Why use moulded items/parts in your work?

To save time in later production.
By producing a simple non-unique piece over and over. For example a chocolate bar.

To have a reliable outcome even on a 'bad day'.
Some days your materials can be extra squishy or you may have very hot or very cold hands which can certainly affect polymer clay. Using a mould means less handling of the material and you know exactly what to expect when your piece comes out.

To make multiple simple parts of a larger piece
E.g. leylandii branch tip which makes excellent Xmas tree branches.

Leylandii mould

To record ideas, shapes and textures
from things you see in your daily life, and from nature.

To make complex shapes
that are difficult and time consuming to make one by one for example human figures and faces, ridged cactus etc.

I recommend the book Making Character Figures by James Carrington. If you have a particular interest in doll making.

To provide one element of a larger piece
making decorative shapes for use in more complex work. You don't have to make the whole item at once. You can make just one element of it. Your finishing is what makes each piece unique.

An example of this is my sweetcorn from my first book Making Miniature Food and Market Stalls. When I first made it, I made each one by the same method. It was laborious and took a lot of strength and control to extrude the clay. I soon realised it would be a lot easier to make a mould rather than making the same thing over and over

Extruded sweetcorn texture

but each cob needed finishing with its husk ... so each was unique. That project was the start of my own mould making. I soon went on to make a pork pie top mould (pork pie is also in book 1). And then I was hooked! My

Moulded figure - stained

Potato rolled on a texture sheet

mum made a moulded figure for her Tudor bed posts.

To create/simulate texture

by making texturing tools. In my case I use textures in miniatures for potatoes, oranges, cheese with a rind etc. Textures can make jewellery and art objects much more interesting and can create surfaces for scenes in animation etc.

Banana crate with handmade bananas

As a base layer for hand finished work

Imagine you want to make a whole crate full of bananas, but bananas are a difficult shape for you to get right. You can choose to spend a lot of time making

Banana bunch in first half of a 2 part mould

your first few bunches, for the top of the crate and then you can make a mould for the less visible bananas at the bottom of the crate.

Then there are complicated shapes you want to reproduce but the whole process is so time consuming that you could save a ton of time if you could just get a mould to do half the job.

Grapes from a mould with 'extras'

Miniature grapes can be tedious and time consuming to make but once you have made a bunch you can copy it by using a silicone mould and simply add a few extra to each bunch to make every one unique.

Even smaller fruit made up of tinier bead shapes. For example raspberries and

Master for raspberries made from no-hole beads

blackberries (brambles) can be simulated by using glass or plastic beads on a cocktail stick to make the original. A mould is then made from this original and the fruit can then be made in large numbers using your preferred material.

You will find these ideas in my Miniature Food Masterclass book and my The Miniature Gardens Book.

I've made moulds for a carrot box base layer and also for spring onions. I've made a pyramid of balls for a fruit stall base to add extra singles on top of. In this case I made the shapes using polymer clay but you could just use polystyrene balls of the right size.

For use with liquid clays
See "Moulds for setting liquid materials" on page 56

Liquid materials would simply run without something to contain them. Do note that you have to clean any surface silicone off moulds before using for items that are baked within the mould or excess silicone reacts with your bakeable material. Even after washing the first item your mould may have a crumbly surface, so you may need to make a throwaway item first.

How to mix

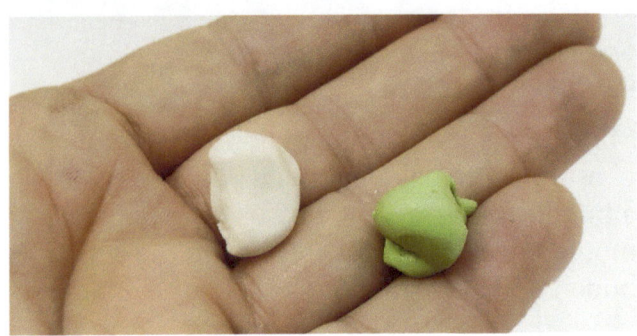

1: when you're ready, take a small amount of each of your two colours

2: mix them together until the colour is perfectly mixed with no streaks

3: do this by pulling and folding until it's completely mixed

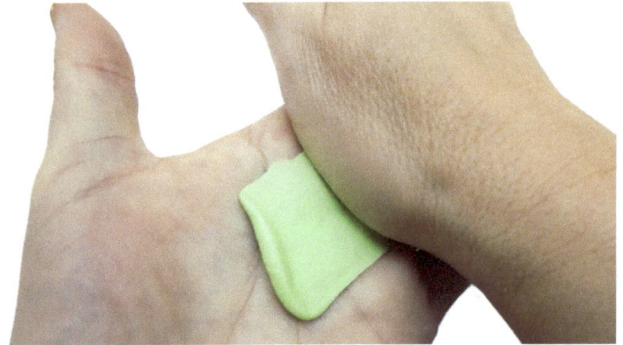

4: stretch it like a baker stretches dough on your palm for a last mix.

Curing time depends on the brand you are using and on the heat in your working environment. It can also be affected by how old the material is. An older material may take longer, or may not cure at all. See "Problem solver" on page 75.

What can you mould from?

Shapes and created forms that you find around the house or see on your travels, including decorative elements from other people's work (N.B. with a careful adherence to the principles of copyright and the moral aspects of to what extent and in what context you 'borrow' from other people's work. More comments about copyright can be found where appropriate in the book. And on "Copyright issues — moulds" on page 70)

Your own sculptural work.

Bits that nature generously provides you with.
The first project to make a cauliflower floret is an example of this.

Right! Let's get started with a simple, one sided cauliflower mould.

Quick start projects

Beginners quick start project – cauliflower floret

You will need
2 part silicone mould material (see suppliers list)
A piece of cauliflower or Romanesco cauliflower.

Small cauliflower floret

Before we start playing with all the things you can do with silicone mould material, let's get straight down to getting a feel for the material. Many readers will already have tried this so do bear with me while I bring beginners up to speed.

Choose a cauliflower or Romanesco floret that is undamaged and has a nice round shape. It also has to be small enough for your project. If you are working in 12th scale it should be only a couple of centimetres across. Of course you can easily go down in scale to really tiny sizes since nature is so fractal in this case. You can trim a slightly larger floret to size by pulling away extra bits that might spoil the shape. The most important thing is the definition of the individual micro florets within your bigger piece. It is worth remembering that the way you 'gather' the modelling material when you are moulding from this mould means you can make the mould from a piece that is slightly large for scale.

Hold in mould material

Now here's the very important stage that makes all the difference to enhancing (exaggerating) the texture. Leave it to dry out a bit! This makes the gaps between the mini florets more defined. Form the material into a little mound on your work surface. Simply press your floret into the mould making material and form a wide shoulder (this is to make it easier to flex). You don't need to bring the mould material right round the floret because of the way you use this mould. You just need to get the surface texture. Hold the floret still for a minute or two or until you are sure that it will not simply fall over. This might depend on the setting time of your material and how soft it is in its mixed but uncured state. Leave to set.

Finished mould

One little caution, fresh cauliflower juice on the hands can affect setting.

Polymer clay pressed into mould

Squeezing the 'stem'

Making the cauliflower

Simply press the creamy coloured mix into the mould and pull out. Then shape the stem and at this stage you can decide how big the 'curd' is going to be just by pressing more into the stem for a smaller curd. Pull away any excess clay leaving a stem of around 2-3 cm.

I surround my caulis with 'caned' leaves. These are in my The Miniature Gardens Book

Miniature cauliflowers with leaves

and a simpler form in my Making Miniature Food book. You can of course bake these and glue on paper leaves afterwards. The leaves are also veined using a 2 part mould but we'll come to that later!

Take away principle

Drying flower, leaf or vegetable parts can make their shape more clearly defined. In this picture of a Romanesco mould the one on the left was made from a dried floret one day later. The difference is subtle but the mould material has been able to settle into the gaps between each tiny section thus enhancing the definition. The item moulded from this mould is therefore going to be just a touch 'sharper'. The smaller the scale you want to make the more important it is that you get some definition so, for example, if you are making 24th scale you really would want to allow a smaller floret to dry and separate a bit. This is because the smaller the scale the more you need to go into hyper reality to leave people knowing what your miniature is. A little white blob may be interpreted as a cauliflower in context. But you want to leave the viewer in no doubt!

Romanesco florets and moulds

Miniature Romanesco

Borrowing forms from everyday objects

Simple texture plates

Silicone texture mould from heavy sandpaper. Introduction to returning to the 'positive' shape by moulding from the first mould.

Until now we have been making negatives (moulds) from our 3 dimensional positive masters. Now I want to flip this idea to make the original texture into the texture I want from the mould. I want to make little indentations in my oranges and potatoes so I need a texture plate. I've been using sandpaper but its a bit spikey and can get very dirty very easily. I want a slightly more subtle texture that I can use for orange skin. This will be similar to the original texture but softer, as the air trapped inside will tend to round off the points. My other use for this texture shape is to apply random brown 'dirt' dots when making miniature potatoes. You can of course use the sandpaper in both cases but the effect is spikier on the orange skin and in the case of the potatoes, using dusting powders I want the powder to come from the peaks and not the holes in this texture.

Get a sandpaper of the largest grit you possibly can. Often these are to be found in the professional and power tools sections of your DIY shop.

Mix your mould material and press into the sandpaper. Leave to set.

Then to make the positive texture sheet, you need to do the 'double step'. That is to say make a second mould from the first mould to get back to the 'positive'. Use talcum powder or cornflour as a resist. Apply it then pat it back off the surface.

Second generation mould from the first

Put a second layer of mould material over the top. See "2 part crochet bunny mould" on page 24

Griddle plate Project

Bolt thread texture plate.

I use a lined texture sheet to make various vegetable textures including the stems of celery. And I use a distressed version for carrot lines.

The master for the mould is simply made by rolling the thread over polymer clay. I had bolt threads without a head to do this. If your bolt has a head you should roll it at the edge of a cutting board or bench so that the head doesn't stop

First mould from heavy sandpaper

Thread texture master

Thread texture mould

the bolt touching the clay. Roll in one swift movement or you will get a bumpy texture. Bake the clay.

Take your texture mould from this master by simply pressing on a thin layer of mould material.

Using thread texture to paint lines

This can be used to make a nice lined texture in your work.

Grilled fish with griddle marks

IMPORTANT steps

You will need talcum powder or corn starch dusted onto your first mould to act as a release. Wear a mask!

You could also make the first step from scrap clay and bake. Then mould from the clay without the need to use a release.

Be aware of the lost definition because although in this case we want this effect it can be an unwanted problem for other work and can be quite common with the second generation of this technique.

You can also use it as a griddle line maker by dusting with brown powder to colour cooking fish, steaks etc.

One more step

If you roll the thread the other way you suddenly get chocolate bars!
If you want to make a mould for individual bars, simply cut your polymer clay texture to the size of bar you want. I always cut at a slight angle as it looks more realistic.

Thread texture rolled in 2 directions forms a chocolate pattern for further moulding

Moulds from your own work

Dabbers, printers and impression tools (imprinters/stamps)

Getting practised in drawing on clay.

Try your signature. While we're at making imprinters, why not try making your signature as a moulded rubber printer/imprinter.

Draw your signature onto polymer clay or wax with a very small ball tool. Try to keep your pressure even. If the depths vary too much you will not get an even depth of imprinter and it won't print well. Don't worry about the excess clay that the ball tool produces. You can clean that up after baking.

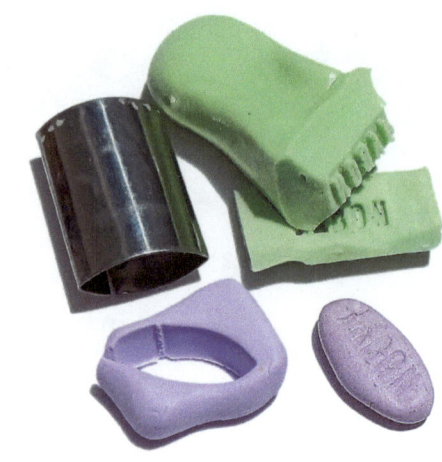

Soap imprinted (in Spanish)

Bake the polymer clay and then make an imprinter with a handle. If you used wax, make the imprinter directly into the wax. Note, I found that I did not write my signature as evenly as I should so it didn't print very clearly.

Words - soap

To make the original of this I used an oval cutter from a leather cutting set and letters from a little rubber name tape printing set where you can put the words together in the mounting. Take a mould of that and then make an imprinter mould from that original.

I used my larger rubber letter stamps to make vegetable crate printers

Draw your own signature

Print (before removing excess mould material edges)

Print (after edges carved away)

Vegetable box printers

Parmesan and Parma ham stamps

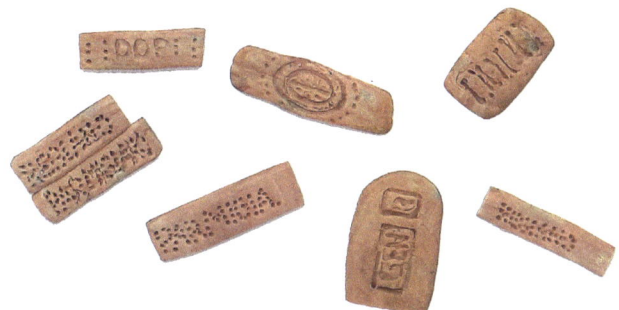

Several masters for Parmesan imprimenters

Parmesan with imprinted rind

I wanted even smaller letters for this and looking at the real things the words were created as a series of dots so I spent quite some time writing in dots. I made each separate element as a different imprinter by working on small bits of clay and then making the imprinter from the baked clay. The problem you have here is making the mould material 'fall away' from the dots so that the edges of your imprinter don't take too much chalk powder and deposit it on your work making a rather messy look. You may need to carve these edges away.

Parma ham

Parma ham imprinted

For the Parma ham I needed concentric ovals so I sacrificed a couple of my very smallest circle cutters. There are some available really cheaply which are repurposed electrical parts sets. You can find these online. I pressed mine into the oval shapes I needed. I did the original work on to polymer clay and then wrote lightly inside. This was a long time ago and I did it very simply at the time. I scribed the crown shape into the clay too.

Parma ham D.O.P. imprinter

The important thing for making printers is that you are careful about the depth of your work. It has to be regular as parts which are less deep won't produce a printing edge. Only the deepest parts will print. This is difficult to get right because you are working blind. It can help to use a tiny ball tool to scribe with so you can see the depth of the ball. Or you can mark on a dental tool.

Moulds from fabric

Moulds from fabric

Jumper project

If you don't have a friend who can make you some mini clothes try cutting up old fine knitting into the shapes you want. You can then make moulds from that.

Cut out fabric from some fine knitting (an old sweatshirt or jumper or some finely knitted socks). Glue them to a piece of card and then make a mould from them. You can make these things thin and flat and then fold them. I decided to make a fisherman style jumper from the fabric in one of my old but finely knitted jumpers. It had matted in places, in others

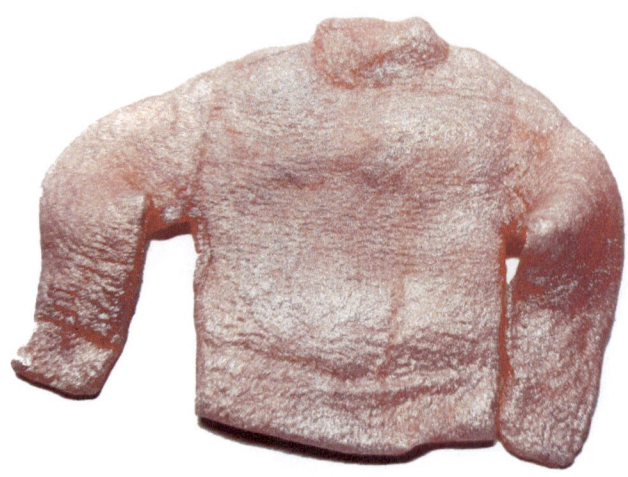
Jumper made from Metallic Cernit

not so much. I used it ribbed side up for the cuffs, waistband and the neckband which I made doubled over to give it extra strength. I used the inside knit pattern for the body and arms of the jumper. The pink one is pearlised clay moulded directly from the mould, taken out and rearranged before baking. The purple one is baked semi liquid clay mix (Goo). Of course when baked in the mould the item has a very static shape whereas when solid clay is moulded it can then be rearranged to make a pleasing 'thrown' down or 'folded up' look.

I decided it was best to use semi solid 'Goo' in my mould for this purple one. It's very important to remember to clean the excess

Pieces from an old jumper

... glued to a card backing

Mould material pressed into the surface

Jumper made from polymer clay / liquid clay 'Goo'

Applying Goo to the mould

Knitted socks and mould

Moulds from knitted miniatures

I asked a Spanish friend who lives in the UK (Lula Miniland **instagram.com/lula_miniland**) to knit me some miniature baby clothes. She made these lovely little items which I moulded from. I then made a master mould so that I could do saleable reproductions. You can take moulds from other people's work because it's

Finished jumper from liquid polymer mix

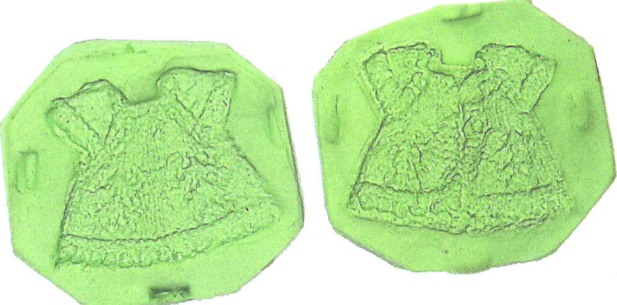

2 part mould from a baby dress by Lula Miniland

silicone off your mould before using it to bake inside. I forgot the first time and got a very powdery looking surface. This can still happen anyway. A mould becomes more useful for baking in once it has given up all its excess silicone and air. So expect the first one or two items baked in a mould not to be perfect and to have a somewhat crumbly matte surface.

You can make other garments glued to paper and moulded. For polymer clay artists try using 'caned' polymer clay for making the resultant moulded items.

You can also use lace to make collar and cuffs moulds for polymer clay dolls.

not for the same thing. For example a solid jumper is never going to be a real jumper but it might look like one so it's important to ask permission first!

You can use a one sided or a two sided mould for these, depending on where the item is going to be seen. If it's always on a surface and you are never going to see the back you don't need to make a back for it. Making a two part mould gives you the option of hanging the article on a hanger. You don't have to knit 2 pairs of anything. You can mould from just one for both … if it's two sided.

2 part crochet bunny mould

You will need
Talcum powder
Polymer clay carving tools

Moulding obviously knitted or crochet items can be fun. Here's a 2 part bunny mould I made from a little bunny by my friend (and patron) Karin Sorensen. As you can see the mould material takes up the really strong crochet details and leaves very little material in the threads. You don't need to talc the bunny/object before making this first half. Lay the object on its back and bring the mould material up to the edges. It's important you don't have a huge dip round the edges as the second half of the mould shouldn't have to fill too many dips round the object. For example, I put a little extra between the legs to make sure it came half way up the bunny's legs.

Wait for the first half to set before making the second half.

Remember talc is necessary to stop the two parts of the mould sticking together, but if you use too much it will blur the sharp detail so add a little talc and then pat it off again without rubbing it off the mould material. When making the second half make sure that you fill any awkward areas first. This might mean some pressing into the edges of the fabric in this case, then adding the rest of the moulding paste. In a complex shape like this following the contours will save having to use too much expensive mould material.

To make a bunny from the mould I filled the 2 sides then pressed Fimo into each side pressing down well to make sure there is polymer clay in all the small details. Press the mould together really well. The stiffer the material, the more firmly you will have to press.

After the first pressing you can open and remove any extra clay that has squidged out using a scraping tool.

Applying talc to first part of mould

Patting excess talc off the mould

Ensuring mould material gets into all the corners

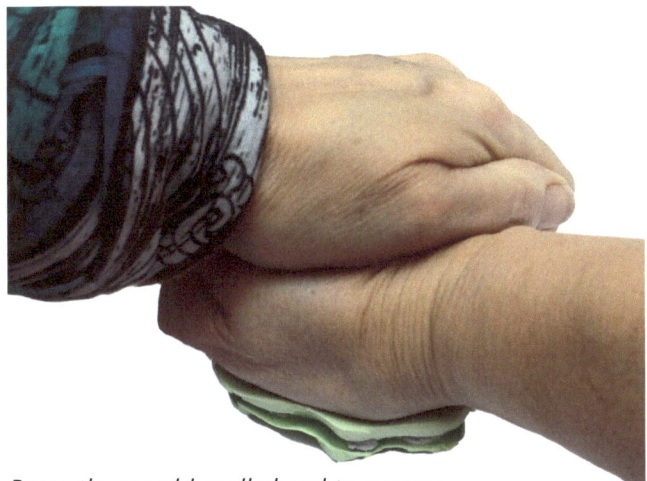

Press the mould really hard to ensure excess clay escapes into the edges

Refining

You might have to do this more than once. It's ok to have a little edge that you can carefully carve away before or after the clay is baked, but it shouldn't be thick or it will leave an ugly line. Disguised it looks just like a sewing line.

Scrape off the excess clay

A note about this project

The bunny arrived at the 11th hour for this book so my first experiment had to go in. If I were to do it again I would place it face down first and ensure the join came further towards the back to be less visible. I would also have taken the bow off the ear to make it easier to change from 'girl' to 'boy'. And you could take off the facial features and change them after moulding. She's a grumpy little bunny! You can work on the line both before and after baking. If you make a crochet texture 'dabber' it would help. Be careful not to handle a soft clay bunny too much though!

Flex the mould to release

Moulding From Nature

The generous plant world
(Take a walk on the wild side)

When you are looking for leaves that are smaller versions of larger species here are some of the types and qualities of leaves you might look for.

1 simple leaf with even, symmetrical veins

2 long arrow shaped leaf with even, symmetrical veins

3 reverse heart shape leaf with symetrical veins and obvious sub-veining

4 five pointed leaf with veins that radiate from a central point with sub-veins

We did the cauliflower mould right at the beginning of the book. Now let's explore what nature can provide further, and what use you can put these forms to.

Nature is very economical with its forms and I'm endlessly fascinated by the fractal nature of our wonderful world so there are many plants which produce leaves which have a variety of leaf sizes, some of which are a 12th scale version of themselves. There are plants which produce faithful little pumpkins and a tree which produces a usable pattern (for altering) for a pineapple (and also a hedgehog), but I haven't found the names of these yet, just the fruits for sale at miniature fairs. While walking in Spain I found the carmine plant which produces perfect little fruits which look very similar to satsumas, but by far the most exciting is the fractal form of the Romanesco cauliflower who's tiny whorls are each minute versions of the whole. It's very easy to reproduce in miniature simply from a mould made from one of these pieces. It's not just plants that reproduce forms though, creatures are also modelled on each other by tricks of natural selection as you will see later.

Flexible moulds (for leaf veiners etc.)

Time to go for a walk or enjoy your own garden, investigate nature, get a new appreciation of weeds!

Remember some leaves have a different veining pattern. For example some leaves have veins which land opposite each other on either side of the central vein and some have staggered veins. Check out the real leaf you want to simulate. Then others, for example vine leaf and squash leaf veins radiate from the stem. When looking around in nature, learn to spot the similarities between small plants and larger plants that have repeating growth patterns.

Simple leaf veiners

Leaf selection
Unless the plant you want to simulate has very small versions of itself (more about this in the centre pages) you may need to look for leaves that have the same basic form. A vine leaf does not have the same shape as a rose leaf for example, but

does have the same basic shape as a marrow or a maple leaf. If you aren't sure and you don't have the real thing to hand, look at botanical drawings which will help you work out the shape and how the veins lie. For example some veins lie opposite each other symmetrically. Some are staggered. Some have heavy subdivisions, some are very indistinct. Bear in mind the scale. If you're working in 12th scale you certainly want to be looking for very small leaves. It's worth taking time to look at the size of the largest leaves on the plant you want to simulate. Dividing by 12 will give you the size of the leaves you are looking for. Also be sure that the veins on your leaf are clearly defined. Avoid any leaves that have very thin feeble or indistinct veins. In miniature making, you need to exaggerate a little.

For this example (see the leaf project on the next page) I've chosen a climbing bean leaf from my garden. The reason I chose it is because it has strong veins as it's a young leaf, the veins are fairly regular and symmetrical.

Although I normally work at 12th scale I've chosen a leaf which is a bit bigger than I normally would. To get a 12th scale leaf you often need to pick the very smallest leaves from the plant just as they appear.

And finally, turning the leaf over, you'll notice that the back has a comparatively stronger texture. If it's summer when you're doing this you will have a wealth of leaves to choose from. If it's winter you might find it a bit more difficult.

Sometimes the best texture/press leaf moulds and 2 part veiners come from the back of the leaf. This is because the stalk parts are more prominent on the back. If this is the case use the back of the leaf to make the first half of the mould then remove the leaf, powder the first half and make the second half of the mould directly from the first half. In the case of using this as a press mould it's this second piece you'll need to press on for a leaf front.

You might also look to see if they are furry or smooth, shiny or matte. The same colour on the front and back or a different colour. Note down the colour (see my Colour Book for more colour details).

Make notes. Take your notebook with you on walks and collect samples of little weeds!

5 *fat arrow head leaf with not wholly even veining*

6 *leaf bract made up of 5 smaller leaves*

7 *leaf bract made up of multiple leaves of differing sizes*

8 *fern shape opposing rather than symmetrical sub-leaves*

9 *single main vein or separated parallel veins*

Very tiny leaves from the tip of a bean plant

Apply moulding paste to the first layer

Imprinters leaf project

Press the back of the leaf into the moulding material and gently smooth it round the edges so that the edges curve away gently from the

Moulding from the back of the leaf

Applying talc as a resist for the second part

mould. This edge gives you extra flexibility for using the mould in several ways.

Leave the mould to set. If you are already an expert mould maker, here's a little tip. Just before the mould sets you can squeeze the edges a bit to make it set even more 'crinkly'.

When this first half has set, remove the leaf. If your leaf was really delicate it could have left a few shreds on the mould. If this happens you will need to remove the leaf bits with your fingernail or if it's really stubborn use a soft toothbrush and water. Don't pick these bits off using anything spiky as you can damage the mould.

Talcum powder the first half lightly. Don't breathe in talcum powder. Use a mask or work outside.

Tap off the excess talc by tapping the mould lightly against your palm or another mould. If you leave too much powder on the mould it can affect the definition. You only need a very thin film.

Make up a similar amount of mould material and cover the first half with this. Flatten your mould outwards, taking up a similar shape to the first half so that you can tell which end is which.

Ensure you start in the middle of the first half and press the mould material outwards until it lines up with the edges. This avoids getting air

Veiner/imprinter with handle

Cut a leaf shape with a small cutter

Leaf pressed between the two parts of the mould

between the moulds. Air would cause loss of definition.

When the mould has fully set, peel the two halves apart. Your mould is ready to use on leaf shapes. You don't need to wash it or use any resist for use as a leaf veiner.

Note: in some cases you need to keep some of the depth as in the case of the chard leaf centre. In this case you can leave the middle stem in by cutting or tearing the rest away.

To make and use a leaf imprinter for tiny leaves

Sometimes your leaves are too small and fiddly to use a flat veiner or to press mould. In this case I make a leaf imprinter. For example for garden plants like my climbing bean plant. This type you can use as a double sided veiner or you can just use the imprinter to 'dab' the texture on to a lot of tiny leaves at once saving a lot of time

Method

Take a small heavily veined leaf of the leaf shape and vein type you want to use. Take a mould from the back of the leaf.

Powder the one sided mould and mix a small amount of silicone. Form your silicone into a teardrop shape and press the base of the teardrop onto the leaf part of the one sided mould. Keep hold of the back of the teardrop gently until it sets. This will take 5-10 minutes.

This method is best for flat sheets of clay with the back a lighter colour than the front. I roll out on the very thinnest setting on my pasta machine. Then thin out even more by stretching and smoothing. Cut out your leaves with a leaf shape cutter (for very tiny leaves I use the Kemper teardrop shape cutter) and put them on to flower foam (EVA foam) then print them, you can then attach wires with polymer clay 'Goo' (solid/liquid clay mix) before baking or use a strong glue like Gorrilla glue afterwards.

You can use imprinters like this as printers for putting extra colours on your leaves too. Either in the veins or on edges for example.

Mushrooms

Gills on a real chanterelle mushroom

The opposite style of imprinter can be made for mushrooms. This is a mould where, rather than pressing the mould into the clay you press your clay on to the mould. In this case you need to draw the gill shapes on to a piece of clay, look at the real mushroom you are trying to simulate.

2 coloured clay sheet

Obviously you need to use my number one rule for miniaturisation: 'simplify and exaggerate' the gills. You can't possibly draw so many gills as there are in real life.

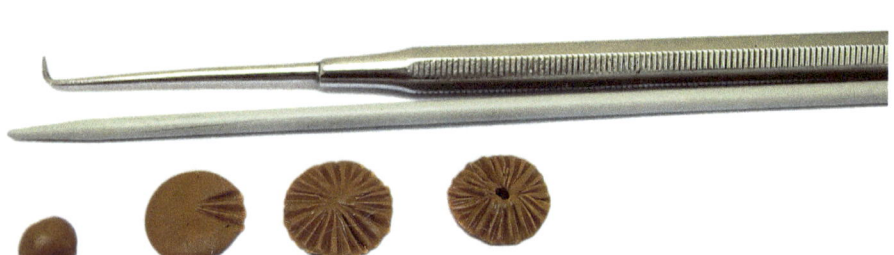

Drawing gill shapes into clay

Press clay into mould

Mini project

Take a small blob of clay. Press it on your baking surface and draw the gills with a fine pointed dental tool or a bent pin.

Draw them in towards the middle point. Then press a ball tool into the middle. Bake the master. You can then make a mould from this master.

When making the mushrooms, squeezing the mould will produce a different shape as in these chanterelles. I add the stems individually.

Squeeze to shape and release

Mould made from master

Making a scene with moulds

Hand made fish for miniature fish / fish shop moulds

Fish mould projects

Making shapes for fish moulds and then moulding from them, couldn't be more simple. Imagine what fun it could be to do earrings from glittering fluttering fish.

Simple assembled fish shapes and mould

2nd generation mould from piled up single fish

Fish crate filled with moulded fish

Use netting to simulate the fish scales. The finer the net, the smaller the scales.

Squid mini project

Make your first squid and mould from it to shorten your work time.

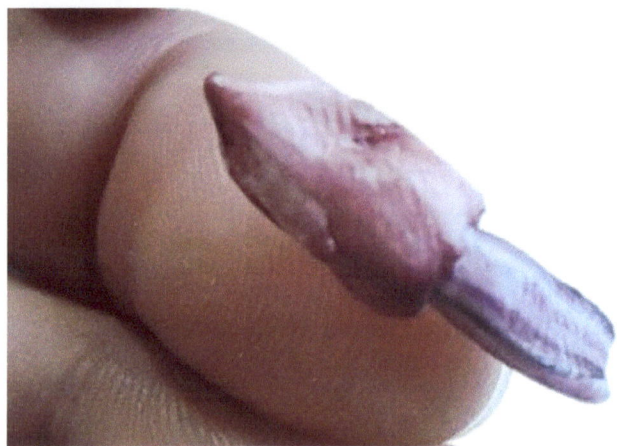

Cone shape with cylinder inserted. 'Wings' pressed

Making the legs

Squid mould

Form a short cone of Puppen Fimo in porcelain colour and cut off so that the end is flat. Push a ball or crafting tool into the flat end to form the body cavity. Flatten the two sides to form the wings. Make several stringy legs, two of which should be longer than the rest. Squash these together and put the top into the body. You may then wish to add eyes. Just form two little balls of clay and push them on to the body with a small ball tool.

Flatten and arrange artistically on a surface to bake. You can make a pile of different squid by making several individually. Or you can mould once from this one, and then make a pile from those arranging each one differently.

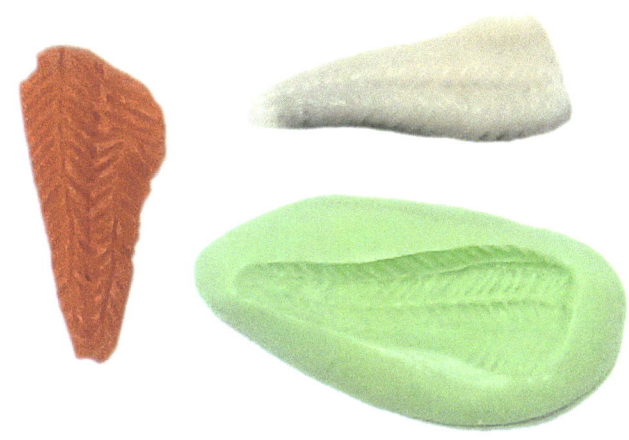

Exaggerated master, mould and finished fillet

the anatomy of the fish you are making to get the general shapes of each part and chevron directions. I draw the sections first and then add the diagonal lines. You can exaggerate these as some definition is lost when making the mould.

I love making these fish fillets with a sliver of caned clay skin pressed on to the back before demoulding. I did the this with cod fillets. Preparing the clay before pressing it into the mould and then trimming. My rainbow trout fillets are another great example of this. Make the double mould from two opposing fillets and then fill with pink flesh coloured clay. Slices of caned fish slices are also used for the skin in this case. For polymer clay caning see my other books e.g. Miniature Food Masterclass.

Squid dislayed on a tray with scallops and oysters

Take away
You can save a lot of modelling time by making only one item and moulding from that in order to produce a pile of similar items.

Fish fillets & kipper

Nice and simple hand modelling, you just need to form a soft fish fillet shape and draw on the surface of the clay to get the flakey texture. It's best if you know something about

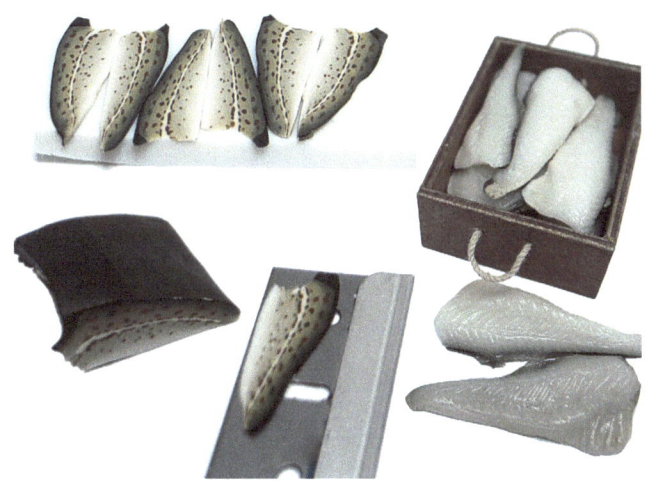

Crates and piles of miniature fish

Crabs, lobsters and crayfish

Crayfish

For this mould I made all the parts by hand. I joined them together and made one single simple mould from the parts. I used natural parts for the more complex bodies of the crab and lobster.

Crabs

I found some little dead baby crabs on the beach. It wasn't possible to mould them perfectly with their legs, so I took a mould from the carapace and from the front claws. Using that original I worked on the results to make my separate pieces The carapace, a pair of claws (joined) and a set of 6 legs. I then made a single whole crab mould.

Assembling crayfish from simple shapes
Mould and finished moulded crayfish

Miniature crabs and mould

Lobster

I used a very small prawn for my original master to make the body mould since they are very similar in shape. The moulding from this master was then worked on in order to get a better 'lobster' shape. And I modelled the claws and legs by hand just as I did when making crayfish and crabs.

Lobster moulds and masters

Miniature lobsters

Octopus mould project

More borrowing from nature's creativity.

You will need

Plenty of mould material as this is a big mould.

ProSculpt or Puppen Fimo or your favourite sculpting clay

Smoothing tool/s

A very small ball tool for improving definition

Coloured dusting powders. You can use artists chalks or powder scraped off artist pastels or make up

Small soft paint brush

Pins and a board which will take pins

AND a real octopus leg!

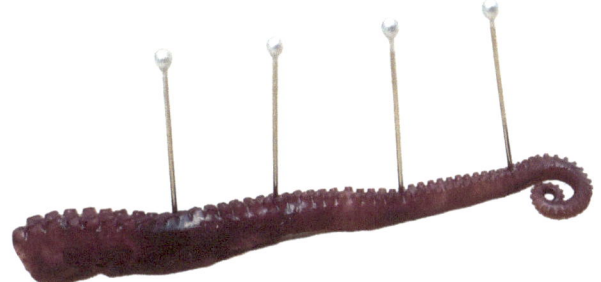

Real cooked octopus leg (end) pinned to a board

Mould pressed down over the leg

Have you ever tried octopus? Did you like it? Personally I find it rather chewy and unappetising except of course in Portugal where they really know how to prepare it! Octopus is a bit of a delicacy at Xmas around here so they sell it in every large supermarket and fish shop and of course the fish man who comes around every week.

It is a fun thing to make in miniature, so if you've ever fancied trying one now is a really good time. See if you can buy it, fresh, fresh cooked or frozen. I made my original octopus mould using fresh but here I give you the project from a cooked chilled piece. It needs to be in really tip top condition and all the suckers need to be undamaged towards the fine tip of the tentacle. Take the very tip off a tentacle. Stretch it out really gently and pin it to a board because otherwise it will naturally lay on its side and you won't get such a good definition on the suckers. The little curly end can be allowed to lie sideways. Squash your mixed mould making material right into the curl and onto the rest of the leg. You may need to work from both sides and meet in the middle, passing right round the pins. I probably used too much of this leg initially and ended up only using the bottom half.

You then need to make eight legs from this single mould. Press the material you are going to use into the mould. To demould you need to flex the mould at the tip end of the leg. Tease the legs out

Remove the leg

of the edge of the mould and remove the rest gently, handling as little as possible. Continue making until you have 8 legs. Cut each leg off to a triangle shape point at each fat end.

Several moulded legs reassembled

Fit all the leg parts together in pairs first. Then add the pairs together, finally putting all 8 together into one. As you can see they need to stay curly otherwise your mould would be enormous! Smooth the joins and finish the middle off with a very small blob of clay. Press a no-hole bead into the very middle to simulate its 'beak'. You don't need to make a mould for the head at all, because you can just use a 'blob' to create that each time. In fact I made a second mould with a tighter curl to make this easier since the ProSculpt didn't bend too easily in my cold workshop. Carefully attach to a base if you wish to make more than one mould from the same master. Your master can break when you remove it. Bake this whole

Octopus mould

octopus master and you can then make a mould from that. This is a very complicated master with plenty of opportunity for getting air bubbles into the mould, so when making your mould you need to make sure you fill the gaps between the legs first so as not to allow any air to stay in under the silicone. If you wish you can add a skirt between the legs but you can leave that out as it gives you the freedom to add it later when making reproductions.

To make my octopus

I like to dust the inside of the mould lightly with coloured powder first. (Always wear a dust mask to do this!) Then form a long strip of modelling material and press it into one leg tearing it off when it reaches the middle. Repeat the process until all the legs are filled. You can then cut off your excess material. I

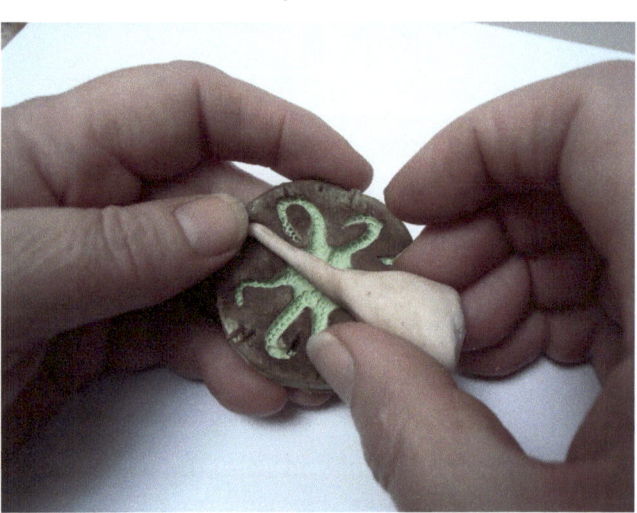

Feed the clay in one leg at a time

use a single sided blade for this but you can use a butter knife. If there is any tearing you can push the clay back into the mould. If you are making an octopus with a head on you now need to make a fat teardrop shape and press it on to the middle. Add a couple of blobs for eyes and a little tube of clay on one side for the breathing hole. Press no-hole beads into each of the eyes. Dust the whole of the upper legs liberally with coloured powder.

Add a blob for the head and features

Remove the octopus gently

Colour with chalk powders

To remove the whole octopus you need to flex the edges delicately just as with the single legs. You can use a soft brush to tease these tiny legs out. When each leg tip is free you can flex the whole mould.

After removing the octopus from the mould you can brush more powder on to the suckers using a brush which is not heavily loaded with dust or a slightly damp brush. This is to add accented edges to the suckers. You can even use a crayon after the octopus is baked to further accent these suckers! Before baking him though, give him a little life by arranging the legs as if they are crawling somewhere. Unless you're making food state in which case upside down and curled underneath is the most usual presentation. You can make sliced/diced octopus leg from the first mould of course. Remember cooked octopus can be an entirely different colour (purple-ish) from fresh (more grey/brown).

If you can't bear the idea of working with a real octopus leg you can make a more cartoonish version by adding tiny rocaille beads to polymer clay. Get the mould right first time though because those beads come off!

Flex to release the legs

Miniature octopus scene, cooked and live.

Using a wavy blade

Seaweed

While I was making a seaside scene I wanted to produce those long ribbons of seaweed that I used to pick up on the east coast of the UK. The frilly edges were going to be difficult but I hit on the idea of using a large wavy cutter to cut a slice of clay and then I could press the centre vein into that.

Bottom halves of 2 seaweed moulds

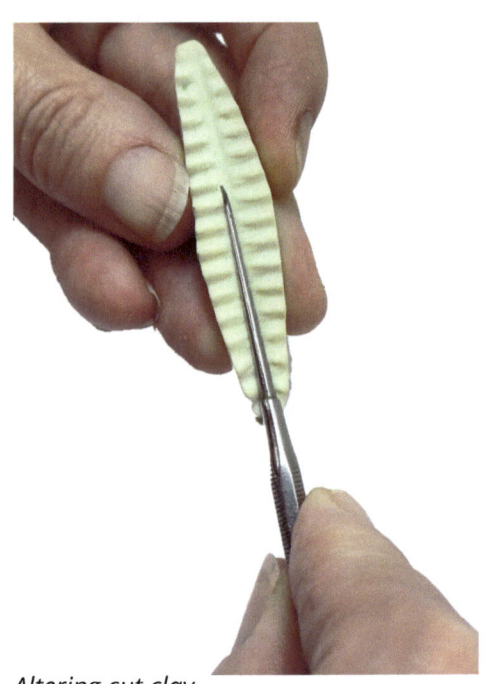

Large wavy blade

Altering cut clay

Miniature seaweed

Making a 2 part press mould (like a leaf veiner) from this shape meant I could roll out very thin sheets of semi translucent clay cut into long sword shapes and press mould them into shape really easily. I then played around with curving a piece back on itself to make a fan shape for other types of seaweed.

Take away

Always keep your mind open to shapes which can be manipulated to give you the form you want.

Wavy blades can also give you press moulds for pleated polymer clay 'fabric'.

Making a mini scallop shell mould from a real larger cockle shell

To make the mould from a cockle shell

All you need to do is push the base of the shell into a mound of moulding material and leave it to set. You need to stand the shall pretty much upright to get the correct shape because of the curve of the shell and don't push it in too far. However you can cut away the excess mould later (diagonally) if you have gone a little deep. Don't use too much mould material because you need the mould to remain flexible in order to release the clay and to accentuate the indentations which you can do by squeezing a flexible mould. Thicker moulds just aren't flexible enough to do this. Add a locator by making a hole in the front of the mould.

Finished 2 part mould set

To make your scallops

You will need a mix of translucent and white (my foundation colour 2) and a little added pearl clay I recommend Doll Fimo porcelain instead of the trans/white mix and Premo for the pearl but any brand will do as long as it's not too soft since modelling requires some stiffness.

You will also need a medium large size ball tool 4-6mm would be good and a soft, small, short paint brush. Some pearlised powder and some browns & ochre dusting chalks or paints.

Make tiny balls of pearl coloured clay. The size of the ball would be around the size of a peppercorn or a very small pearl!

Whole shell base in mould material, locator added

You will need a second half to your mould and you can make this by dusting with talc and making a push mould type second half. Make sure the handle is squared off and not smooth to make it easier to hold on to.

Small pearl size ball of clay

Ball of clay flattened with a ball tool

Press this ball of clay flat into the base and then press in a little more with the ball tool.

Press the second half on starting the pressure at the base of the mould and making a slight rolling movement press the mould fairly hard.

Note: if the polymer clay sticks, dust the base of your mould lightly with your paintbrush using pearlised powder. This will act as both a release and colouring. Don't overdo this or your scallop won't stay in the mould at all. When dusting clay with powders I advise use of a face mask.

Press second mould into the first.

Colour if wanted

You can dust the top and bottom edges very subtly using grey/brown and/or ochre chalk powder at this stage. Alternatively you can do this after baking.

Take the top half off and squeeze the base mould only very slightly to release the shell. You can use your soft paint brush to help release the shell.

If colouring the other side, make subtle lines across the width of the shell. You can change the colours of these dusting powders according to your design as shells from some regions have different colourings through pinks, purples, ochres and browns.

For whole scallops you would need to make the underside fairly flat with a bit of texture.

I recommend baking all your half shells before adding any scallops to them. I make a scallop cane for the 'meat' and both glue the scallop in, and add a 'wet' look using Liquid Fimo, before baking again.

Remove gently from flexed mould

Of course you can make similar moulds for other small shells including mussels and clams. There are specialist suppliers who sell very small seashells. You can of course take a trip to the beach and see what you can find. Take your mould material with you as the tiniest specimens are always delicate and might get crushed on the way home.

Miniature scallop crate, scallop centre canes and mould

Oysters

To make a master for an oyster mould you need to cut several teardrop shapes on very finely rolled polymer clay. Stack them. Press with a craft/dental tool in a couple of places and lift the edges of the 'laminates'. Bake before making your mould.

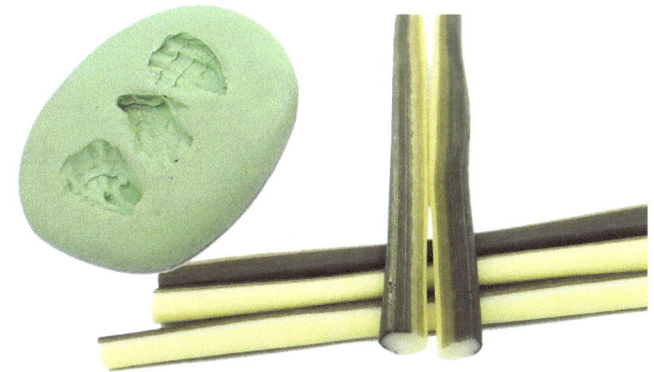

Oyster mould and oyster centre canes

Small teardrop cutters

Laminates lifted with a dental tool

Miniature oyster shells with slices of cane

Moulding Reference Charts

Moulding Reference Chart

Plants that yield elements that are smaller versions of themselves			
Cauliflower and Romanesco cauliflower			
Tiny new fig leaf to make make miniature fig leaves			
Baby chard leaves from the very centre of the plant			
New climbing bean leaves			
Grape vine (smallest leaves)			

Plants which look like miniature versions of other plants				
Mimosa tree fronds for palm fern			
Poke berry (take care - poisonous!) for satsuma			
Coriander seeds for walnut shells			
Putka pods, large make a great squash/pumpkin mould			
Putka pods, small, make a great impression mould for the tops of large Mediterranean tomatoes			

Plants which look like miniature versions of other plants			
Bougainvillea miniature flowers & calyx make a nice flower mould with stem and also a top for peppers			
Flowers of pine trees produce tiny cone shapes			
Leylandii sprigs for Xmas tree branches			
Various cactus and succulents have similar small versions or very small parts in the middle which can be used to make moulds			

From the seaside and from seaside shell shops			
Octopus legs - using the tips for miniature versions (see project)			
Tiny starfish from shell suppliers			
Shrimp to make lobster moulds (claws & legs hand modelled)			
Mini crab carapaces (claws & legs hand modelled)	*this mould taken on site*		
Shells you can find on the sea shore or in shell shops			

Textures from nature			
Stones, pebbles, sand for rocks etc.			

Manmade things you can mould from			
Lace elements for doyleys and fabric effects (liquid clay)			
Metal findings for cake decoration (liquid clay)			
Miniature drill tool bits			
Drill tool burrs to make flowers (liquid clay)			

Manmade things you can mould from

Altered shapes from cutters (gingerbread men)			
Ball tools, working into fresh mould material to make formers for stencilled or paper flowers etc.			
Ball tools altering a fresh mould for extra deep texture			
Bottles, bottle caps etc. to make formers for baskets and planters			
Extrusions used as texture			
Buttons, beads and pins for cakes, bread etc.			

Your moulding ideas			

Your moulding ideas			

Moulds For Liquid Polymers

Moulds for setting liquid materials

Over the years there have been many times my mind has wandered down creative paths taking one logical step after another and finding, or making the tools to help. I've wanted to mould in Liquid Fimo (or sometimes semi-liquid gooey mix of solid and liquid polymer clay) for certain effects. My earliest explorations were in making jellies and cheesecakes in moulds with lollies and then on to rocket lollies which meant using several colours. When I needed a shape for a rocket lolly I realised a cross head screwdriver tip took me half way and I could work on that shape after making a first mould in order to get to the final shape I wanted. That led me to making ice cream cones. All these tiny things were much more easily made

Moulded berries on a moulded cheesecake

Ice lollies and ice cream moulded from Liquid Fimo

taken from miniature jelly moulds. I then went on to making berries to decorate those desserts, using seed beads as masters. I realised you could multi-layer your materials for the cheesecakes and that led me to play around

with a liquid material both for translucency and for ease of getting it into the mould.

For the ice cream there were at least 3 types of ice cream top possibilities.

Here they are for you to play with:

Soft scoop. Use a blackhead remover (yes I know!) to scoop some polymer clay balls out. The fact that the scoop shape has fairly thick edges means that it doesn't cut too cleanly into the clay and leaves those same raggedy cracks

Making berry masters

Ice cream mould masters and mould

that you get in real scooped ice cream. Bake that and use for the master

Machine piped (smooth) ice cream. You can make a carrot shape of clay and twist it into an ice cream shape. Bake and use for the master

I made a mould … to make moulds from my original masters as I wanted to sell the moulds. In the end my mould maker master was too fragile and so that particular mould never got to market.

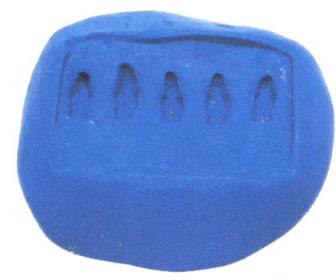

Jelly baby mould

I also enjoyed hand making the masters for jelly babies for use with Liquid Fimo.

All these Liquid Fimo ideas i feel sure would also work with resins, although I haven't tried them

Working directly into a fresh mould with drill burrs

There's one final shape for ice cream tops.
Machine (star shape nozzle) piped ice cream. You can use an icing nozzle and pipe some yourself in soft clay, bake and use as master. Or you can use a drill burr. Drill burrs have many uses as mould makers. I started by making flowers with them. Then I moved on to little cake icing swirls. Then I went really tiny and had a go at teeny 'midget gems', a favourite sweet icing topped biscuit when I was a child!

Midget gems made with moulded icing

Liquid Fimo and oil paints and powders

Cakes aren't really my 'thing' but I have made and taught cake decorating using moulded elements from jewellery and eggcraft findings.

Top Tip
Open your mind to possibilities whenever you see something small with a useful shape or texture. Sometimes you are led by that shape to create something. Sometimes it's the other way round and you are looking for a shape that will fulfil a need.

Project: how to make a master set of false teeth for moulding in Liquid Fimo

(Saving your work in stages and exercising your care and patience!)

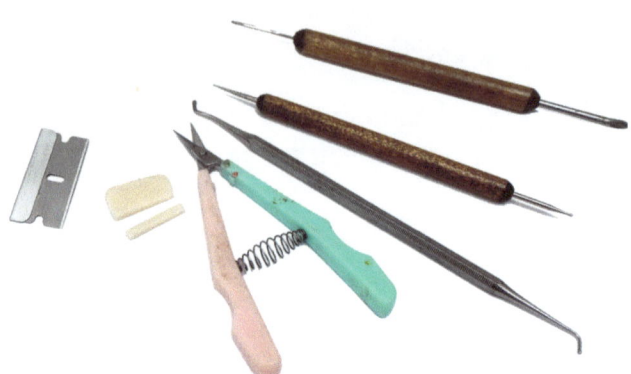

Simple tools

Here's a project for moulding in multiple layers which would be more difficult in solid clay. False teeth moulds. These amused my dentist greatly when I gave him a set and I was even asked to make a lot of them for a dentist convention.

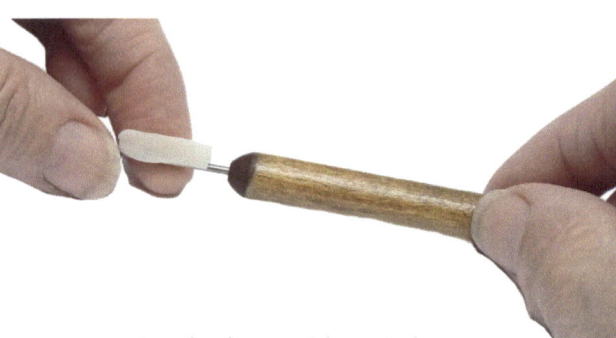

Forming a triangle shape with an indent

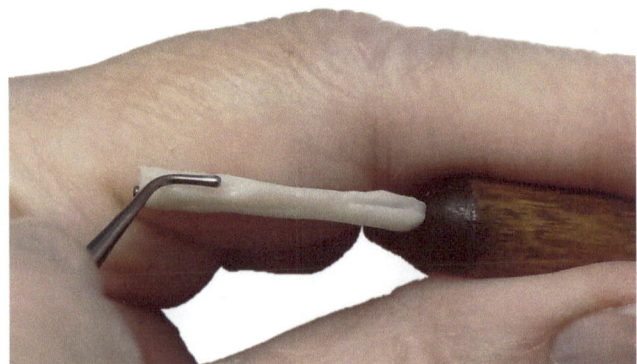

Flattening both the sides for the back teeth

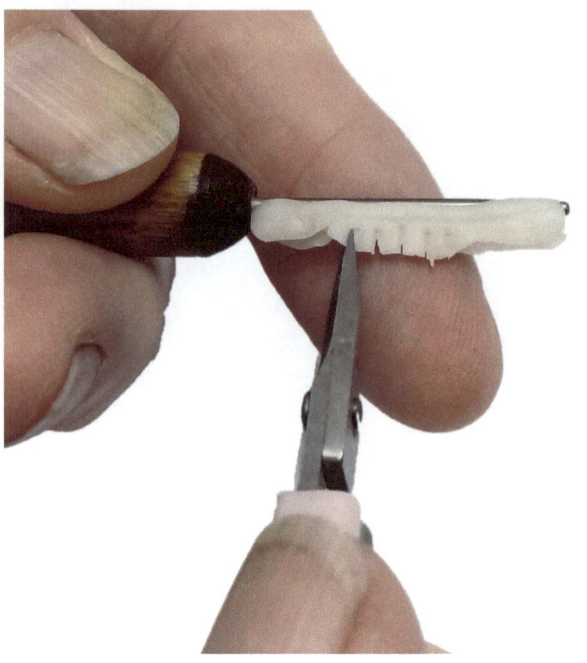

Snipping the clay for the front teeth

You will need:
Firm sculpting clay such as doll Fimo or proSculpt
Liquid Fimo
A set of oil colours
Squeezy bottles with fine tips (modellers glue bottles or vaping bottles etc.)
Your favourite modelling tools. Could be dental tools! Small scissors and a single sided blade

You need to measure the length of the entire set of teeth. If you need a clue, measure round your mouth from the back teeth to the back teeth and take a little off that and divide by 12.

Form a very small deep triangle shape (a bit like a tall Toblerone) on a round tool or fat needle. Decide how many teeth you want and use a pair of embroidery scissors to snip into the top of the clay remembering that the front teeth are wide then the next two sets are narrow. The final teeth on each side are wide and flat. Draw a simple line with a craft tool to show the margin between the gum and the teeth. At this stage do not worry about your teeth not looking realistic! Curve the set round into a horseshoe shape. Cut any excess off.

Bending the formed teeth and cutting off the excess

New ideas:
If you want to save the shape at any stage just bake it and make a first generation mould. Later you can make a second generation from this mould. This is a good stage to make a mould if you want to make really perfect work because you can walk away.

At any stage you can save the work you have already done by making a mould. You can then produce multiples of this shape to work on until you get a really perfect one.

If you want to however, you can carry on with this work but you risk destroying it and having to start again.

Filling the mould with white then later with pink

The next stage is to refine the teeth and the gum margins. Now you need to think about whether this is a top set or a bottom although TBH I usually do them pretty much the same at this stage. The back teeth need to be squashed down a bit and the centres should have a cross in the middle. The canines (3rd set) are more pointed and all the front teeth are more flattened and refined. I usually reduce to 3 back teeth on each side on each part.

The top set needs an arched palate, the bottom set doesn't, so you do need to make 2 sets. Also technically the top set should be able to overlap the bottom. So, it needs to be slightly bigger.

When you make your final mould don't just make one. This kind of liquid clay project lends itself to mass production.
IMPORTANT. Don't forget to wash the moulds really well as any remaining silicone will react with the liquid polymer.

Making the teeth
Mix just a little white oil paint in Liquid Fimo. If this looks too white you can add a touch of ochre. I added a little pearl powder to mine too, but it had to be very fine. You don't want glittery teeth … or maybe you do! Make another mix of pink. False teeth margins are fairly translucent but more pink than standard flesh pink.

Use a bottle with a nozzle to 'inject' the white colour into the bottom of the mould. Make sure that there aren't any air bubbles as this would leave holes in the teeth! Bake in the oven at Liquid Fimo temperatures for 10 minutes. Bring the moulds out, and while they are still hot fill with pink. As the moulds cool you can use a finger and a little kitchen roll to press each mould. This brings a little of the material out but not the bit that the heat has set to the edges. This leaves a pleasing indentation in the 'dentures'.

A pile of false teeth moulds

Several sets of miniature false teeth

Of course, with all bake-in moulds it's a good idea to make multiples of the mould from the master, to make it worth your while putting the oven on. So these are really all ideas for production moulds.

Flexible Formers

Flexible formers

Reversing the process

In this project we take a shape and make a mould from that shape then produce the same shape again. This idea utilises the flexible quality of silicone moulding paste to provide a support armature which will not absorb glue, will hold pins and will flex to pull away from the work made on it.

Basket former

Here I found a beautiful bowl shape which I realised would translate well to a basket shape if squashed. This is one example of where it is just on the right side of acceptable to use someone else's work for a completely different item. It might have been possible to reproduce this kind of shape without the original artist's work, but taking my cue from this form gave me a really beautiful stepping stone to make my work easier. I added some string to the pot shape to make handles, by temporarily glueing it on so that I had a permanent mark of where the handles needed to be.

Mould taken from Carol Mann bowl

This shows how easy it is to use a shape from a different artist's work to make your own work which is a completely different item, and so doesn't count as a copy. There is a fine line in copyright, and this is admittedly only just the right side of it. You shouldn't use your mould to reproduce a bowl however. That would be stepping into the wrong side of copyright. You could use card or paper or polymer clay to make your own shapes or there are some lovely shapes of plastic cosmetic caps and bottle tops you might try. Keep your eyes open for great shapes!

Press your mould material over the whole cap/bowl. And make a rim of approximately 1cm. It can help to draw in your surface where you expect the material to spread to.

Reverse the process (a mould from a mould)

You will need to reverse the process to make a flexible former from that initial mould. Drill a hole through the base of the mould right in the centre. This is to let the air out. Add 2 string handles to the edges of the mould. You may need to make holes for these and glue or pin them in. Dust the inside of your first mould with talcum powder and carefully fill with mould material making sure you concentrate on the inner edges. Any air bubbles will spoil the mould.

How to use a basket former

You will need string, pins and some fabric if you want to line the basket. You'll need to make a pattern from the basket shape to make the liner.

Please note: *be careful not to push the pins right through the mould as they may stick out and cause injury.*

Use string that is 1mm - 2mm (1/32" to 2/32") thick. I like hemp cord very much as it doesn't have loose fibres and it comes in a good range of colours. The heavier the cord, the quicker making the basket will be; the finer the cord, the longer it will take.

If you are lining the basket, glue the fabric piece together round the mould first. Hold it down with pins pushed lightly into the bottom of the mould.

If you are not lining the basket, don't worry the glue will come away from the mould.

Pin the cord into the centre hole

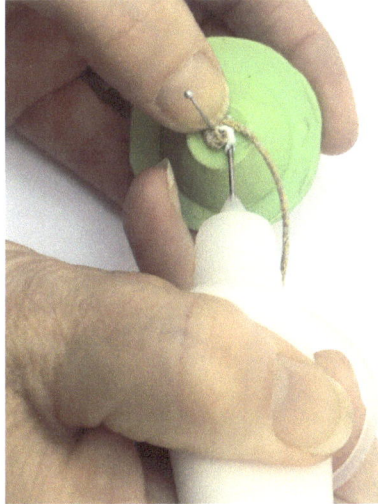
Apply glue with a fine nozzle

Continue glueing and winding

Form handles on the last loop

Start by pushing the end of your string into hole made in the top of the mould and pop a little glue around it. Make one small circuit of string before adding a pin to hold it in place. Put a line of glue below this string and wind around again. Push the string up against the previous loop so that the glue sticks each layer firmly to the one before. You will get glue on your fingers but it will just roll off as it dries or have a lint free cloth to keep wiping your fingers on.

Continue until you reach the handle marks in the mould. If you wish you can pin as you go. Certainly pin if you need to stop. You can remove these pins at any time. Pin the string at each end of the handle leaving a loop to simulate the basket handle. Continue round until the next handle and repeat the previous step. Then cut the string at approximately 3cm from the last handle. Separate the remaining string into its 3 strands and cut one strand short and another one even shorter. Glue these on in the normal way tucking any sticking out bits into the glue. This should make a neat finish. Leave in a dry place for a couple of hours at least, overnight if the place is cold or humid.

To remove the basket from the mould, first remove all remaining pins. Then simply squeeze gently but firmly to flex the basket. This helps it to release. Then press the edges away from the rim of the basket and ease the mould out.

Although you can use the basket open for apples etc. it looks even nicer when used as a shopping basket. You simply squeeze it into shape. You can use a clothes peg to hold it firm until it is fully dry if you like. You can make the handles more secure if you wish by sewing round the edge of the handles into the next layer of string. Any obvious remaining glue and fabric can simply be trimmed away with scissors.

Beach bags. Use a cosmetic lid to make a mould and use the same winding technique as with the baskets, When you come to the top edge make a loop handle on each side, holding the edges of the loop with pins.

*The flowers in the basket and on the hat were made using my flower stencils.

Former made from a bottle top

Mould and materials for a hanging basket

Hanging basket and planters project

Making planter formers

The idea of 'stealing shapes'. Simple moulds and formers to get you used to moulding.

You can try the same trick as I used for the basket using plastic spray bottle tops etc. You can make your own silicone moulds from these tops. To construct larger items I prefer to use silicone mould maker as a former to work on top of. You can also use it for polymer clay etc. because most of them you can put in the oven at polymer clay temperatures (check clay temp).

The very simplest way to make planter formers is to scour your house for bottle lids etc. which have a shape you like. Make a mould from that, and then take a mould from your first mould, turning the negative mould back into a positive, but flexible, shape.

This hanging basket former was made with a half polystyrene ball glued to a disc. I made the mould former from that and then used talc as a resist before filling that first mould to reproduce the original shape.

You can reduce the amount of mould material used by indenting at the back but don't remove too much or the form will be too flexible and it will be difficult to use.

If you are a woodworker you can turn your own originals. if you have a 3D printer you can print them or if you have time and patience you can form the original shape yourself.

How to make a hat former

I made the hat mould from an original (positive) master in polymer clay using 2 circular cutters. One for the hat body and one for the brim. I reshaped each very slightly to be a little bit more oval than circular. I cut the shapes out of the clay and stuck them together smoothing the joins. I took a mould from that (negative) and then made a positive from it.

Mix your two part mould material and cover the hat shape, carefully starting at the middle and covering the whole shape to the edge and downwards to the brim and over the edge so the brim edge is inside the mould. This is your negative mould. You need to make another mould from this to get back to the original shape.

Coat the first mould liberally with talcum powder (do not inhale - use a mask) and tap the mould to remove any excess

Make a hat former with circle cutters

Adult 'boater'

Hat master

Child's hat with curved crown

powder. Mix more mould material and now fill the centre first allowing more material to push the edges out. Then spread the rest of the material to the edge of the first mould. Make a mark across the edges of both the moulds. When this has hardened, remove from the first mould. If you want to make a 'production line' you can make more of the formers from the first mould.

For a smaller childs hat former, you could use a hemispherical wooden bead or half a polystyrene sphere for the crown and cut out card or use a small circle cutter with polymer clay for the brim. For a witches hat, a cone. You can use these formers with string and glue as with the baskets

The hats look best made with a much finer string than the baskets. Or you can use polymer clay shapes baked on to the mould, or even fabric soaked in PVA dried on the mould/ former.

The reason these formers work is because the PVA glue peels off the silicone when you flex the mould and /or the hat formed on it, both due to its flexibility and the oils in the silicone.

These hats look excellent with organza ribbon tied round, and left hanging over the edge a little.

Boater dressed as a Morris dancer's hat

Almost Impossibly Difficult Shapes

Moulds for (almost) impossibly difficult shapes to take up really fine details

Bathroom set moulds project 1-part mould.

A miniaturist friend wanted moulds for 12th scale bathroom products. The massager was a big challenge and I found several different ways of doing it. One was to make a lot of long drop shapes of clay. These were then set into the heart shaped base. The easiest is to push mould material into a mesh until it produces the length of 'bobbles' you want.

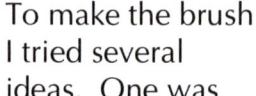
Clay extruded through a piece of net

In all cases I realised I needed to make moulds in 2 parts. Modelling the handles was a matter of using oval cutters of different sizes for the oval ones and hearts of different sizes. The handle was modelled from a flat wooden cocktail stick. Lots of stages of moulding and some carving and sanding was needed for this project.

Clay extruded through gauze

To make the brush I tried several ideas. One was to extrude clay through a piece of very fine mesh. The second was to use a very deep pile velvet. Finally I settled on using a bundle of bleached coconut fibre which I cut a flat end on and liberally covered with PVA glue. This was left to dry before cutting through again making a fairly coarse brush appearance (see the previous page).

The massager was the most difficult and once again I tried several different ideas. Extruding clay through netting, through metal mesh and through a clay extruder (which did I finally settle on? I don't remember!) The soap shape was a simple oval leather cutter. Leather cutters are often smaller than normal cutter shapes and stronger so less likely to warp.

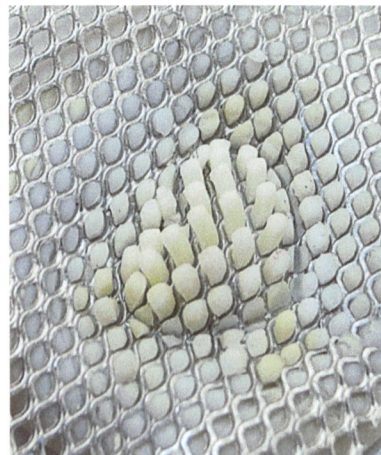
Clay extruded through metal mesh

Bathroom accessories masters and moulds

Extrusion techniques

In some cases you can find a shape that can be extruded in soft clay or in mould material.

I've made bell peppers by extruding clay through a clay gun 3 or 4 lobed flower shape, rounded off and sculpted the top and bottom ends. The master is then baked and moulds taken from that. The halves were made from this shape cut in half. To make the inner shape it's important to make an actual empty bell pepper shape, add any detailing (seeds, shapes etc.), bake it in the mould and then make the second half from the filled mould.

To make the pepper halves from this mould you can make a Skinner shaded thin sheet (like for the leaves) so that the inside is whiter and more translucent. Press the clay in lightly with a ball tool. Put the second half over and squeeze lightly. Then you can open and cut off any excess.

Extruded chilli pepper (3 sided blossom die)

I've made cactus by simply extruding and stretching Minitmold through star and flower shaped cutters to make the first shape. I have then moulded from that shape and sculpted the ends myself. In both these cases you need to cut into the first mould to release the original. To make sure it closes back together perfectly aligned don't cut through the last milimeter or if you do I've found it possible to 'sew' a hinge into the mould using elastic thread which is generally available at import shops craft departments.

Cutters used as extruders

Second mould taken from extrusion

Take away
Moulds can hold really fine details which can otherwise be lost when copying and transferring textures and decorative motifs that you literally couldn't reproduce by sculpting. Silicone moulds are particularly good at this.

Refined shape produces the third mould

Copyright issues – moulds

This is an important section and will appeal to those who have truly good and artistic intentions.

I am not a lawyer and these are simply principles I live by. They are not comprehensive and anywhere I suggest there may be a grey area you should exercise caution and your own moral judgement.

Copying other people's work and passing it off as your own is ungenerous, uncreative and may even be illegal. You have been warned!

On the other hand, because I teach, I expect people to make work that is similar to mine so I expect and welcome people making work that is like mine based on my techniques. You can also make work from the moulds I sell, because that is my design to sell and you are implicitly 'licensed' to use it by buying from me. However I have a hard line that I draw to make it very clear, because copyright is a knotty subject. If you pass the techniques off as your own I do get a bit stroppy, as inventing techniques and teaching is what I make and sell! Other artists may well not wish you to make and sell copies of their work even if they have published them. It's always best to check.

More specifically on the issue of mould making:

Do not directly copy anyone's work using a mould to take their hard work and pass it off as your own or to sell in any form. There is one caveat to this. You can take moulds from part of a work if the work you make from this is indistinguishable from the original in either form or function. There may be cases in the second where you are still in a grey area. For example if you take a mould from an artist's 3 dimensional artwork to use as a coaster, no problem. However if you want to make a Grolsch bottle as a miniature or an earring, technically you still need permission. Many artists are happy to say yes especially if you give them credit. But they always appreciate being asked. Win - win! If they say no, take their refusal graciously. Use your judgement. For example earlier in the book I use forms that are clearly for one use and completely turn the use into something else. I have no problem with this at all. The fact is I always credit the original artist and the original use when I can find them. If anyone tells me the name of the original artist for example of a metal filigree, I will happily credit them with the design as used in a mould I might take to make embellishing forms.

Moulds For Surface Effects

Using moulding and pressed patterns for surface effects

Miniature ceramic or faux cast iron planters from polysyrene shapes.

You will need
A found object 'shape'. This can be any shape that you think might be suitable including small bottles, bottle tops boxes etc. If you want the polystyrene bead effect you'll need to look for something made from polystyrene!

Cernit metallic clay or similar rolled out to a thick sheet.

Soft silicone ended modelling tool
Single sided blade

I also used some pre-made stencilled polymer clay forget-me-nots as a decoration.

I've used the lovely Cernit Metallic range in many of these experiments. The first one was Cernit Metallic haematite and Cernit Metallic rust (with a little added gold).

This time I'm using the inside of the mould to form my planters.

The following ideas came to me while making a planter mould from a piece of polystyrene packaging material. The shape was pleasing, but the bubbles of polystyrene had gaps between them which meant that the mould material entered between the bubbles making raised parts in the mould. Of course these raised parts become indentations in any clay used within the mould.

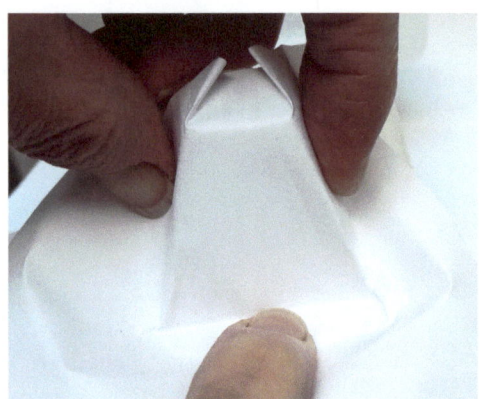
Paper pattern making

To make my first planter I made a pattern piece in paper by pressing it against the sides and creasing the corners. I could then cut the pattern out. I then made a solid pattern out of some polymer clay because I knew I would be using it a lot.

I rolled out some haemetite coloured Cernit clay and stuck some of my previously stencilled and baked forget-me-nots to it. As they are also polymer clay I didn't need any glue.

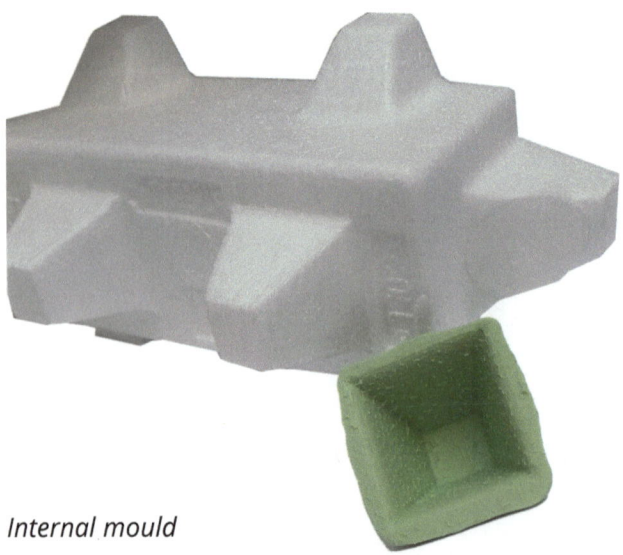
Internal mould

A sheet of Cernit Metallic haemetite

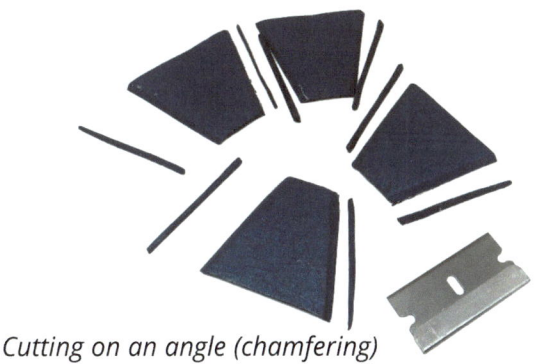

Cutting on an angle (chamfering)

After cutting out the shapes I chamfered off the edges (cut off diagonally) so they would fit together well in the mould.

I used some of these little triangular shapes to press into the joins to strengthen them. I used a silicone modelling tool to press the pieces together.

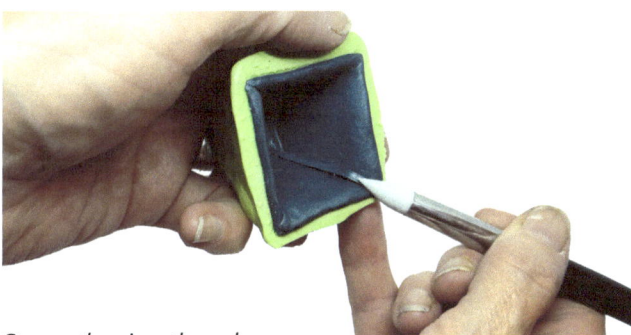

Strengthening the edges

I then cut a tiny square and filled the base. It doesn't matter if this is too big, it will simply hold all the parts together more firmly.

I then cut a piece of dry oasis to shape to support the inside of the pot against the side of the mould. You can use kitchen roll or aluminium foil or even blind baking beads or lentils (don't eat them afterwards though!).

I used Oasis because I was going to use it as a planter anyway and so it could stay in situ and simply be covered in scenic soil material for planting.

Oasis to hold the shape

N.B. Although I personally have found that Oasis does not melt in the oven under polymer clay temperatures, my oven is situated in a separate craft room. I cannot guarantee the safety of any materials under heat, and so include the picture just by way of explanation.

Here the texture is visible

The finished pot does, of course have the original texture of the polystyrene.

These can be disguised by filling and making a second generation mould but I thought I would play with the effect...

Filled with stencilled irises

I realised I could fill these afterwards if I wanted, either with the same material or with gold colour to look like Japanese 'kintsugi' or with a rusty colour so that it looks like rusted iron.

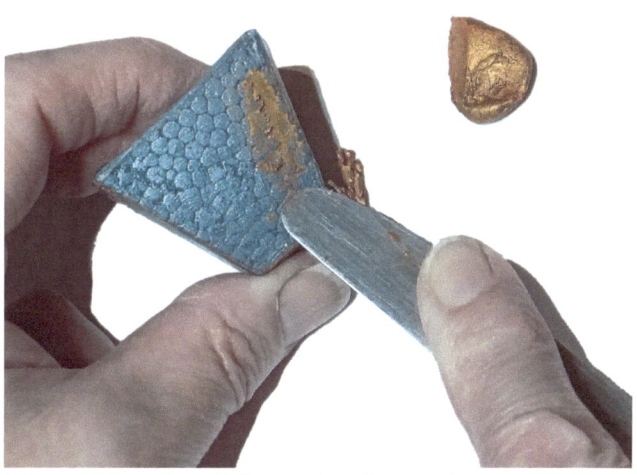

Filling the surface holes with polymer clay

In my second attempt I filled the baked clay with soft clay in rusty colours, using a butter knife and baked again. Then I sanded with progressively finer sandpaper until I got the effect that I wanted.

In this case I left it matte as I liked the appearance of slightly rusting cast iron.

Baked, finished pot

Then I decided to play with other polystyrene shapes

The polystyrene ball shape makes a lovely round pot. I used a very 'bad' extruded shape for this one. It had very loose beads and so lots of indentations. You can sand and then shine to get interesting marble or granite effects.

Top tip:
Keep your eyes open for shapes in packaging!
You can also try making moulds with other fillable surface effects by carving out textures on the master.

Polystyrene balls moulded and the tops cut off

A thin skin turned inside out

A thin skin turned inside out can be used to texture inside the pots or any surface. Play around with polystyrene and see what else you can make!

One caution. It is quite difficult to make the walls of a bowl regular thicknesses especially with smaller moulds. Start playing with bigger shapes and progress as you get more confident. These tricks make wonderful beads too!

Shining using a nail sanding block

Problem solver

Mould material not curing (vulcanising) at all

The material is too old. If you've had your mould material over 18 months it could be past its effective dates. However I have heard that if you put it in a very low oven (100-120 degrees centigrade) you can force it to cure. I don't know how true this is as I've never had any material long enough for it to stop curing.

It's too cold in your house/workshop. Try warming your hands and your immediate area. Or you may have to wait a little longer for the cure to happen.

Some material affects silicone moulds causing poor setting. Anything containing latex like latex gloves etc. does seem to cause problems. Masters made from Du-kit seem to have problems at the surface nearest the master This can cause mould material to come off the mould onto your clay.

To avoid this you can coat your master liberally with varnish but this would have a negative effect on fine detail so, all in all it's best to avoid materials which cause this problem by using a non-reactive material when making masters for moulding

Mould material curing too quickly

You were too slow to get the material on to the work or get the work into the material (whichever your method). Try a slower cure material or be more prepared/more practised.

It's too warm in your house/workshop. Wait until a cooler time of day, use an air conditioner or cool both your hands and the material. You can pop small pots of it into the fridge for half an hour so that you start with cooler silicone.

Note: *Minitmold is a very fast setting material so you might need to start with a slower one or start off making only very small moulds to make sure you don't waste too much in practise.*

Lost definition through air bubbles

Shiny patches in your mould indicate that air bubbles have got in.

When a mould from a master or the second part of a mould has set, examine it carefully. If any part of your mould or texture plate comes out shiny you will have lost definition at least or worse you may have introduced visible errors. It is very unlikely (not impossible) you will be able to repair this and your best option is to start again. Certainly don't ever waste material making a second half of a flawed first part of a mould. Better to make a new first part until you get it right. If a master produces air bubbles consistently in the same place you may need to drill an escape hole into the master. An extreme example of this is on my octopus mould master where I had to drill holes all the way round. Sometimes a gently curving wall to the mould master can cure this on its own (like my sweetcorn mould master).

Another way to minimise air bubbles is to work from the centre of the mould outwards allowing air to slip out sideways. Or in the case of very complicated moulds, again like my octopus master (the one I make my saleable moulds from) we have to press a little material into each of the places where air might collect first. My husband is actually better at making from this master than I am!

Check that the mould does have all the detail. It is worth trying to repair a single simple bubble in a simple mould. For example if there is an air bubble in the corner of a plant pot mould you can put a teeny bit more mould making material in and press the plant pot in again. This may work but may leave you with shreds of the fix which leave an imperfect finish.

Your item does not come out of the mould cleanly

Either your mould is too complicated or has too many undercuts. With a really complex shape (such as a cactus with many ridges) each ridge is an undercut so as you flex your mould to let the piece out it can squash each of these.

Or the mould material is too flexible or not flexible enough. Once again this can cause the mould to dig into the clay rather than release

Or your polymer clay or other material is too soft or too hard. Too soft material will deform as you try to remove it (see both the above reasons). Try leaving the item in the mould in a cool or very cold place such as the refrigerator for an hour or two. Hard clay may fracture, so condition the clay well.

Chart of setting times

fill in with details of your favourite materials at your local temperatures

Brand	Info	Warm setting	Cool setting	Notes

Suppliers

Amazing Mold Putty

https://www.alumilite.com/silicones/amazing-mold-putty/

Pinkysil Putty Silicone Rubber

https://www.barnesnz.co.nz/addition-cured/pinkysil-putty-silicone-rubber-1612

Silicona En Pasta "Rápida" Igum

https://resinpro.es/product/goma-de-pasta-rapida-igum/

Gédéo Siligum

https://en.pebeo.com/catalogue/famille/gedeo-modeling-materials/766309

Minitmold

https://www.angiescarr.com

Jewellery and egg craft findings, metal elements etc.

https://www.bindelsornaments.nl

ProSculpt

Available on Amazon and Etsy

Puppen Fimo & Liquid Fimo

At your craft shop or Fimo supplier

Clayaround (Penny Vingoe) UK supplier of polymer clays and related materials

https://www.clayaround.com

Cernit
https://www.clay-and-paint.com

Seashells etc.
https://www.facebook.com/GriffithsSeaShellMuseum/

And for anything you can't find **The Blue Bottle Tree** has extensive lists of suppliers
https://thebluebottletree.com/polymer-clay-resources/vendors-and-suppliers/

Biography

Angie Scarr is now widely considered as one of the 'godmothers' of miniature food ingredient and latterly botanical miniature making. She considers herself a miniaturist's miniaturist rather than a perfectionist, having spent the larger part of her life adapting, inventing and teaching her own techniques and sharing her knowledge through books, classes and through her Patreon group.

Her early published ideas, though innovative at the time, are now part of the way miniatures are routinely made and her newer ideas continue to inspire. Angie's greatest love and therefore her skill is in solving three dimensional problems and finding short cuts. Sharing that excitement with others continues to be a joy to her and through sharing that delight she continues to have an influence on a new generation of miniature artists.

Because Angie's experiments have often involved finding easier ways of doing things, quite naturally most of those years she has added mould making experiments to her other techniques.

This book is a round up of all of those 'tricks and hacks' with a few bang up to date ideas thrown in as she continues to experiment right into 'old age' … If miniaturists ever age!

For more biographical details and some of Angie & Frank's crazy adventures see her autobiographical book Making It Small available on Amazon as a paperback or ebook.

Thanks & acknowledgements

My lovely patrons who are unstinting in their support of me and without whom I couldn't have got through these last 5 years and written the books!

Mandy Lancaster, Lisa Sones-Peck, Maryse Cuypers, Essie Kenneway, Alexander Baytchev, Christine McKechnie, Marta Terán, Gillian Mason-Thompson, Gail Barlow, Jacquie Hall, Karen Tiberius Rollinson, Robyn Stewart, Natalie Martin-Burrows, Carol Medina, Riemkje Boom-Oosterhof, Kasia Win, Sandi Kluge-Smith, Mary Katherine Myers, Linda Nielsen, Sue George, Sarah Benham, Karin Sorensen, Essie Kenneway,Tara Jane Susie Langworthy and Stephanie Ryan. And, of course, many more who didn't give permission to be named but who are just as important to me. Thank you all!

My patrons have supported me not just financially, each according to his/her ability, but also emotionally. That has been just as important over the last few years.

Many thanks to Lula Miniland for the miniature knitted baby dress and accessories, and to Karin Sorensen for the crochet bunny. Carol Mann the amazing miniature potter who's bowl shape I used for the basket mould.

As always I'd like to thank all my other mini friends past and present who have supported me. Among them the organisers of the many fairs I've been privileged to attend and the magazines I've had the honour of appearing in. The other miniaturists and polymer clay artists who have inspired me along the way, most of whom I've mentioned in other books. You are remembered, even if your names aren't here.

And of course I want to thank Frank who sometimes gets a bit more than he bargained for as I can be pretty demanding as an author when he does all the donkey work as he definitely has in this case. I acknowledge that his name really should be on the front but, bless him, he's a modest soul.

Index

banana	11
basket	51,62,63,64,65
bathroom	68
beach bag	63
bead	11,38,39,51,56,65,72,73,74
berry	56
blackberry/bramble	11
blade	38,40,58,72
brush	68
carrot	11
cauliflower	14,15,28,46
Cernit	22,72
cheesecake	56
cord	62,63
crab	36,49
crayfish	36
crochet	24,25,78
dabber	18,25
EVA foam	31
fabric	22,24,40,50,62,63,65
false teeth	58,59,60
fish	17,34,35
former	51,62,64,65
Goo	22,23,31,56
grapes	11
hat	64,65
ice cream	56,57
imprinter	18,19,30,31,32
jumper	22,23
Kemper	31
kipper	35
knit	22,23,24,78
lace	23,50
leaf	28,29,30,31,46
Leylandii	10,48
Liquid Fimo	43,56,57,58,59
lobster	36,49
lolly	56
massager	68
midget gems	57
mushrooms	32
octopus	37,38,39,49,75,76
oyster	43
Parma ham	19
parmesan	19
planter	51,64,72,73
poke berry	47
polystyrene	11,64,65,72,73,74
press mould	29,40
printer	18,19,30,31,32
ProSculpt	7,37,38
Puppen Fimo	7,34,37
raspberry	11
resist	16,30,31,64
Romanesco	14,15,28,46
scallop	41,42,43
seaweed	40
signature	18
soap	18,68
spring onion	8,11
squid	34,35
stamp	18,19,30,31,32
surface effect	72,73,74
sweetcorn	10,75
talcum powder	16,17,24,30,41,62,64,65
Tudor bed	10,11
undercut	6,76

Patreon
Why I love my patrons

If you've never heard of Patreon before, imagine you could be a 'patron of the arts' in some small way helping your favourite artists to continue working, inventing and teaching in their specialist area. Artists no matter how well known in their field often have no regular guaranteed income and often give away their inspiration for free because until now there wasn't an easy method to gain an income from day to day teaching, support and skill sharing.

This subscription service is an easy way to connect artist teachers with their students and followers, and as a way for the 'patrons' to give the level of support they are comfortable with and receive in return (sometimes personalised) perks such as early access to new ideas, live patron only videos and little samples of work to help you visualise stages of work and qualities of colour. As well as advance knowledge of really new ideas before they ever get to publication. Some ideas of how I made things which never even reach the books which I call my 'daft ideas' for example how I made the awning for the dollhouse shop on the front just using parts from an old umbrella! For benefit patrons I'm also able to send out little found 'things' which might inspire you, or samples of my new tools before they go into full production.

Many thanks to my current 70+ patrons some of who have been with me for several years now. You've all given me courage to start with new things like this book. The Patreon thing has really helped me because it's like having 70 sets of shoulders to lean on. 70 therapists and 70 special friends to share my daft ideas with and see if they work. Or at least are interesting enough for you not to walk away! 70 people who understand that no matter how well known an artist is they still may struggle from time to time. That's worth so much!

www.patreon.com/angie_scarr

Making Miniature Food & Market Stalls

Angie's first book Published by Guild of Master Craftsman Publications. A bestselling introduction to making polymer clay miniature food. This is an updated edition.

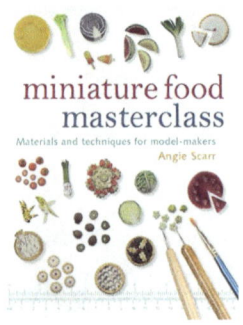

Miniature Food Masterclass

Angie's second book with GMC. Also still a bestseller this one continues the journey of exploration into what polymer clay can replicate.

Other books by Sliding Scale

The Miniature Gardens Book
Have you ever fancied making more than just a flower garden in miniature? Angie gives you several garden styles and lots of new ideas.

The Dollhouse Flower Shop
This book concentrates on the innovative idea of stencilling flowers in polymer clay/liquid clay mix. Some equipment and materials are needed to get started.

3D Pen #1 Fairy Houses and Fantasy Gardens
A handy pattern book for anyone of any age who is looking for a project to make with their 3D pen. Excellent addition to a 3D pen gift.

Your Creative Business
Angie and SEO expert Kira share advice on all aspects of craft business from pricing and marketing through to multiple income streams to help you ensure a more secure future.

Your Creative Business Workbook
To go with the main book or as a stand alone. This workbook helps you decide on your business direction and includes ideas to improve your planning and profits.

Angie Scarr's Colour Book
A small book that asks the big questions about colour realism in polymer clay, helping you towards work that is so realistic it seems to jump out from the rest.

Angie Scarr Miniature Challenges Part 1
Revisiting all the old magazine articles in Dolls House and Miniature Scene and other dollhouse magazines most of which are otherwise out of print.

Angie Scarr Miniature Challenges Part 2
More old dolls house magazine articles revisited. Some with updated information.

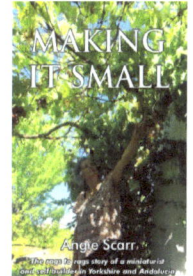

Making it Small- Biography
Angie never lived an 'ordinary life'. When she and Frank met it became less ordinary still. A story of the love of crafts, miniatures, self building and life in a small pueblo in Spain.

The Frugalist
A look at revaluing your time, living better for less and gently preparing for unexpected crises. If life sometimes feel tough this book might just help.

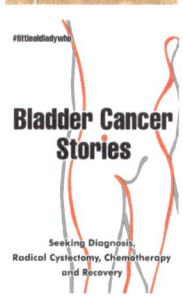

Bladder Cancer Stories
A personal, often humour filled journey through the downs and even ups of radical cystectomy and chemotherapy: back to health and a different view on life after bladder cancer.

www.angiescarr.com

For moulds, stencils, kits, books, miniatures and other craft materials
delivery worldwide

www.etsy.com/shop/AngieScarrCrafts
Our Etsy Digital store for plotter / cutter files. Flowers, leaves, boxes and a flowershop are among the designs.

www.patreon.com/angie_scarr
Support me and get sneak previews of my work and discounts in our shop.

www.facebook.com/angiescarr.miniatures
My facebook page where I let everyone know what is going on

www.instagram.com/angiescarr
Photos of work in progress

www.pinterest.co.uk/angiescarr
Links to my work all over the internet

ko-fi.com/angiescarr
Buy me a coffee

www.tiktok.com/@angiescarr
Video shorts

www.youtube.com/user/angiescarr
For tutorials, howtos and videos about crafts and miniatures

www.ingramcontent.com/pod-product-compliance
Lightning Source LLC
LaVergne TN
LVHW070439080526
838202LV00035B/2667